DALE ROACH

The Servant-Leadership Style *of* Jesus

A Biblical Strategy for Leadership Development

WESTBOW
PRESS®
A DIVISION OF THOMAS NELSON
& ZONDERVAN

Unless otherwise noted, Scripture quotations are taken from the Holy Bible, New International Version. Copyright © 1973, 1978, 1984 by the International Bible Society. Used by permission of the International Bible Society.

WestBow Press books may be ordered through booksellers or by contacting:

WestBow Press
A Division of Thomas Nelson & Zondervan
1663 Liberty Drive
Bloomington, IN 47403
www.westbowpress.com
1 (866) 928-1240

ISBN: 978-1-5127-2730-2 (sc)
ISBN: 978-1-5127-2731-9 (hc)
ISBN: 978-1-5127-2732-6 (e)

Library of Congress Control Number: 2016900728

Print information available on the last page.

WestBow Press rev. date: 03/09/2016

Contents

Acknowledgement

The creation of this book has grown out of a treasure of friendships that have encouraged me to think on the subject of being a leader while at the same time being a servant. I have received a true gift from the Lord in the wealth of relationships he has introduced into my life. I also must express my deep appreciation to Camille Hiott,and Caleb Breakey for their editing skills.

Servant-leadership has been a way of living for many people in my life. I am sure that I would have never thought of this subject or even considered writing about it if it were not for some wonderful followers of Christ in my life. Some of the strongest and most vibrant servant-leaders I know have been the women in my life. There is something extremely powerful about godly women who love the Lord and people in their lives. It is with great pleasure that I dedicate this writing to my mother, Helen, my daughter, Elizabeth and my best friend and wife, Shelley. Over the years, I have watched all of these women explain to me by their actions what a true servant-leader is all about.

"…Jesus called the Twelve and said, "Anyone who wants to be first must be the very last, and the servant of all." – Mark 9:35

Introduction to Servant Leadership

What is the definition of servant-leadership? Is that phrase a contradiction? Can a leader be a servant? Can a servant be a leader? Some may find it difficult to combine the two words. Together, they don't make sense in a culture of self-promotion and self-centeredness. For most people, servanthood and leadership do not go hand-in-hand.

To serve someone else is a discipline that must be learned and practiced. I was born in 1961. To many young people that sounds ancient. Being a little over a half century old does declare that one has some age on them; however, in my life's experiences I have been among people of various generations. In fact, when I was born, there were five living generations of people in my family. I also had the privilege of being introduced to a woman in 1983 who was born in the 1880's. To engage in a conversation with someone over one hundred years old is a privilege I will never forget.

My journey of growing up in the southern United States introduced me to a way of thinking that has somewhat faded in today's culture. I was raised in an environment of leaders who believed in serving other people. This way of thinking was founded upon the teachings of Jesus. Although the term servant-leadership was never used during these early times of influence upon my life, that was exactly the type of behavior that was being modeled to me. The men and

> In the New Testament Jesus completely redefined leadership and re-arranged the lines of authority.

women in my extended family had a solid belief that caring for those around them was a "calling" in life.

In the New Testament Jesus completely redefined leadership and re-arranged the lines of authority. On one occasion, He told His disciples, "Whoever serves me must follow me; and where I am, my servant also will be. My Father will honor the one who serves me" (John 12:26). Jesus made it clear that serving others would produce a reward for those who practiced this behavior. Those Christian uncles, aunts, grandparents, and parents in my life who knew Jesus also knew how to live by His teachings.

Being a healthy leader requires much more than being a ruler or a boss; it calls for dedication and sacrifice. Garry Collins wrote, "Great leaders do not lord their leadership over people, exercise control, and authority, or jockey to get positions of prominence. Great leaders, instead, are servers."[1]

Servant-leadership is a life-long process. Becoming a servant was the foundational plan of Jesus' ministry strategy. It is a practice that takes the proud and makes them humble. If an individual Christian desires to become a leader, he or she must become a true servant. How does this take place? This type of behavior only happens when Christians live in an ongoing, growing relationship with Jesus Christ, who was the creator and perfect model of servant-leadership.

In reading through this book and studying the Scriptures provided, you will find that it was never Jesus' intention to promote Himself. The focus of Jesus' ministry was to proclaim the Kingdom of God. There were times when He miraculously healed someone, and then gave instructions not to tell anyone (Mark 1:44). This type of instruction is a sign of a servant-leader who was not self-promoting. Those who follow the example of Jesus understand that real and honest servant-leadership is all about helping others, not oneself. Thus, community development, a goal that some modern Christian cultures are ignoring and brushing aside, is an important aspect of servant-leadership.

Furthermore, Jesus recruited and empowered other people to help, thereby modeling the importance for servant-leaders to grow other servant-leaders and to avoid isolation. It was never Jesus' intention to work alone. Chuck Lawless wrote in his book *Discipled Warriors*, "Leaders who work alone are asking for the Enemy's attacks." He goes on to say that "we are most susceptible when we are alone."[2]

Becoming a servant-leader requires training from an expert in this practice. Jesus' wisdom and guidance in this area cannot be compared to the instruction of any other teacher known to mankind. We can learn from the lessons and practices of Jesus to help us strive for and embrace servant-leadership in our faith journey. John wrote it this way in his epistle to the early church, "...whoever says he abides in him ought to walk in the same way in which he walked." (1 John 2:6) That "walk" with Jesus that John wrote about calls us to examine and apply the strategy of the Teacher. Tommy Nelson penned these words, "Unless you serve, you will never, ever lead. Leadership's a piece of cake when you learn how to serve. There is no greatness without servanthood. There is no success without submission."[3] The goal of this book is to understand servant-leadership as Jesus taught it and to submit to His teaching, coaching, and inspiration to become servant-leaders.

> "Unless you serve, you will never, ever lead. Leadership's a piece of cake when you learn how to serve. There is no greatness without servanthood. There is no success without submission."
> *Tommy Nelson*

CHAPTER 1

The Creation of Servant-Leaders

Jesus called them together and said, "You know that those who are regarded as rulers of the Gentiles lord it over them, and their high officials exercise authority over them. Not so with you. Instead, whoever wants to become great among you must be your servant. - Mark 10:42-43

What do you think about when you think of Jesus Christ? There can be little doubt that Jesus has made His mark in this world. The question "Who is Jesus?" has responses as varied as the population that makes up this planet. There has never been another individual who has had such an influence on so many cultures, languages, and countries.

Jesus was very clear about the values and standards He wanted His followers to learn. In His teachings He made it clear the Kingdom of God operates with principles very different from those of the world. The behaviors and attitudes Jesus taught of were so different from other religious teachings at the time, that even His disciples did not always demonstrate an understanding of living out the servant-leader lifestyle.

> Jesus was very clear about the values and standards that He wanted His followers to learn. In His teaching He made it clear that the values of the Kingdom of God are very different from those of the world.

The Foundation of Servant-Leadership

To understand how radical Jesus' teachings were on leadership, it's important to examine what authority and power looked like at the time of His ministry. For thousands of years, the Jewish people were primarily subject to foreign rule with only brief intervals of self-government. At that time, the Romans ruled the Mediterranean. There was a very clear hierarchy of power: Jewish autonomy was subject to King Herod and the local Roman government who in turn reported to Rome (Emperor Caesar). The Jews were suspect of Roman government, which controlled everything. For example, even though Jewish citizens were under the authority of the Jewish court system (the Sanhedrin), all capital punishment decisions were sent to the Roman government.

Not surprisingly, the Jews had much hatred and mistrust of Rome. And they knew what "power" and "authority" looked like. Jesus, however, turned His disciples' normal worldview of leadership and headship upside-down. It was the Passover before Jesus was to be crucified, at the evening meal. Judas had already left to betray Jesus, and Jesus got up from the meal, took off his outer garments and wrapped a towel around His waist. Then John writes:

> "…he poured water into a basin and began to wash his disciples' feet, drying them with the towel that was wrapped around him." – John 13:5

The disciples were baffled. Washing feet was something normally done by a servant. Peter declared Jesus would never wash his feet, to which Jesus replied, "Unless I wash you, you have no part with me" (John 13:8b). When Jesus was finished, He then told His disciples:

> "I have set you an example that you should do as I have done for you. Very truly I tell you, no servant is greater than his master, nor is a messenger greater than the one who sent him. Now that you know these things, you will be blessed if you do them." – John 13:15-17

Jesus' challenge to His disciples was not about the superficiality of washing feet. It was the call to serve others with a Christ-like attitude. Jesus was setting up His followers for God's heart for ministry: seeking the benefit of others—an instruction and challenge for believers throughout all generations.

When James and John argued over positions of authority and power in Matthew 20, Jesus challenged them to adopt a different attitude. They were to be servants to those they were to lead. For James and John, this was not instinctive; leaders led with power and the sanctions that made power possible. But Jesus' model was different. How different from the world's definition of leadership!

Jesus' goal in modeling this type of leadership was to prepare His disciples to be able to propel God's kingdom on earth when He was no longer with them. The disciples needed to be prepared to multiply leaders who lead *according to God's heart*; they needed to lead as Jesus led.

Perhaps this is why some of His last words to His friends before leaving earth were a challenge to do likewise, "to observe all that I have commanded you" (Matthew 28:20).

When Jesus called people together and taught them from the Mount, he was challenging them to behave in ways that showed results. Jesus called His followers to demonstrate the character of humility, regret and sorrow for their sins, gentleness, peacefulness, and a willingness to endure persecution for the Kingdom of God. His lessons were based upon a life that is conducted by a spiritual power greater than one's self.

Not only did Jesus teach about the attitude of one with a true servant's heart, He declared them to be blessed if their lives demonstrated a heart of humility. In teaching us about a servant's attitude, Jesus established the foundation of servant-leadership, which according to Jesus, begins with developing a healthy heart (Matthew 5:1-11).

The Dynamics of the Beatitudes and the Servant Leader's Heart

The Sermon on the Mount may be the Bible's utmost leadership lesson plan. Jesus retreated to a hillside to reveal the true standard of servitude and ultimately of Kingdom life required of all who belong to Him.

When Jesus was speaking to this mass of people He was reflecting upon the group's dynamics. As Christ looked over the mass of people, He saw a variety of individuals with unique talents, skills, and gifts.

"Now when Jesus saw the crowds, he went up on a mountainside and sat down. His disciples came to him, and he began to teach them. He said:

"Blessed are the poor in spirit, for theirs is the kingdom of heaven.

Blessed are those who mourn, for they will be comforted.

Blessed are the meek, for they will inherit the earth.

Blessed are those who hunger and thirst for righteousness, for they will be filled.

Blessed are the merciful, for they will be shown mercy.

Blessed are the pure in heart, for they will see God.

Blessed are the peacemakers, for they will be called children of God.

Blessed are those who are persecuted because of righteousness, for theirs is the kingdom of heaven. (Matthew 5:1-10)

Those who are "blessed" have private lives aligned rightly with the Lord. The core of the word "blessed" is the idea of "approval." The type of leadership Jesus was introducing was one based on serving others, and, according to Jesus, is the only kind approved by God. These lessons spoken to a large group of people on a hillside in Galilee set the foundation for what a true servant-leader looks like.

The Poor in Spirit

The "poor in spirit" are individuals who recognize their own need for spiritual guidance and leadership. It is a person's inner realization of need, of emptiness, and of dependence on God. To be "poor" does not mean financially needy, but spiritually destitute. They have admitted their need for God's mercy and turned away from their confidence in themselves. For the Jews, the poor in spirit were those who understood they could not rely on their physical connection to Abraham to save them. The poor in spirit were those who had come to see themselves as spiritually impoverished and in need of God's grace, mercy, and forgiveness, and recognized their true condition before God. It is the exact opposite of being rich in pride.

These people are most often those who are seeking the wisdom and guidance of others. Jesus assured those listening that recognizing their weaknesses would be a positive asset for them, and necessary for entrance into the Kingdom of God.

Those Who Mourn

"Mourning" in these verses does not mean "Blessed are those who are gloomy, unhappy Christians!" but those who are sorrowful over sin. The apostle James wrote, "Grieve, mourn and wail. Change your laughter to mourning and your joy to gloom" (James 4:9). James was not talking about sobbing for the sake of sadness, but of the result of realizing one's sinful state before God.

When Jesus addressed this concept of mourning, he was speaking about those with an empathetic heart. Not everyone is sensitive to the needs, hurts, and challenges of other people. Those who mourn have sensitivity in their approach to life. Christ assured those who mourn that brokenness would not be ignored. In fact, what Christ was teaching is that those with a sensitive heart will receive benefits. The psalmist writes in Psalm 34:18, "The Lord is near to the brokenhearted, and saves those who are crushed in spirit," and in Psalm 51:17, "The sacrifices of God are a broken spirit; a broken and a contrite heart, O God, you will not despise." Those who realize their sin and are sorrowful will be blessed, and this is a necessary characteristic of a servant leader.

The Meek

Another word for "meek" is "gentle." This is an opposite spirit to that of the arrogant and patronizing Scribes and Pharisees and their followers. D. Martyn Lloyd-Jones says, "A man can never be meek unless he is poor in spirit. A man can never be meek unless he has seen himself as a vile sinner. These other things must come first." To be "meek" does not mean to be weak. In contrast, one who is meek does not use power for selfish purposes. Meekness is controlled strength. It is power completely surrendered to God's control. It is an attitude of heart in which all energies are brought into the perfect control of the Holy Spirit.

Meekness says, as in the words of Jesus, "yet not my will, but yours be done" (Luke 22:42). It is a God-honored character trait, and a fruit of the Spirit (Galatians 5:23). A person who is meek is never bitter, malicious, self-seeking, self-promoting, arrogant, or vengeful. Meek people are those who work in the background. It is never their goal to be self-promoting or to be put in the limelight. Their goal is to be humble, quiet, and supportive. Jesus assured these individuals that they would receive rewards for their service. This type of quiet, humble, servant-leadership is foundational to the ministry of Jesus.

Those Who Hunger and Thirst for Righteousness

These people carry the distinct character of a Christian desiring holiness above all things. The psalmist spoke to the passion for righteousness called for in this beatitude when he wrote, "My soul is consumed with longing for your laws at all times" (Psalm 119:20). Job, whose soul was being severely tested, understood this. He found his strength and nourishment in the proper food: "I have not departed from the commands of his lips; *I have treasured the words of his mouth more than my daily bread* (Job 23:12, emphasis added). Jesus was teaching that men and women of God will be blessed when they continually long to know Christ's righteousness and live their lives with a constant desire to be conformed to His will as a starving man longs for food or thirsts for water. Only this type of person will be truly satisfied.

Hunger and thirst are bodily cravings that must be satisfied in life. For Christians, this "hunger and thirst" goes beyond the physical. Those who hunger and thirst for righteousness are those who yearn for things done in the right way. Jesus assured these followers their hunger to see things done right will be satisfied. Righteousness may not always be easy to see or find. However, Jesus said that those who intentionally seek it out would find the good in life.

Those Who Show Mercy

These individuals are those who have the ability to show grace and forgiveness. They are actively compassionate and concerned about other people in need. The apostle Paul repeatedly talked about the mercy of God. In his letter to the Romans, speaking of God's mercy to both Jews and Gentiles, Paul states: "Just as you who were at one time disobedient to God have now received mercy as a result of their disobedience, so they too have now become disobedient in order that they too may now receive mercy as a result of God's mercy to you. For God has bound everyone over to disobedience so that he may have mercy on them all." (Romans 11:30-32) This is the heart of God.

Kingdom servants reflect in their own hearts the heart of Jesus. They are "others-focused." What they have received by grace they in turn share with others. Disciples of Christ actively demonstrate sympathy for other people by extending the necessary resources to successfully comfort and strengthen them—including to those they lead. There are many places of service, businesses, volunteer groups, and congregations where mercy and grace are needed characteristics that are

> The promise to those who show mercy is simple - they will receive mercy. This is one of the greatest promises of the Beatitudes.

hard to find. The promise to those who show mercy is simple - they will receive mercy. This is one of the greatest promises of the Beatitudes.

The Pure in Heart

Jesus said that the pure in heart will see God. These people are those who have not allowed their minds or their hearts to be clogged with the baggage and trash in the world.

Look at Jesus' contemptuous verdict against those who appear "pure" on the outside as practiced by the Pharisees:

> "Woe to you, teachers of the law and Pharisees, you
> hypocrites! You clean the outside of the cup and dish,
> but inside they are full of greed and self-indulgence."
> – Matthew 23:25-25

To be pure in body is good, but according to Jesus, to be pure in heart is best. If a person is pure in heart, they will be pure everywhere. To be pure in heart then means to be pure from the inside out.

The heart is the control center of a person's entire life. The book of Proverbs tells us to watch over our hearts with all diligence, "for everything you do flows from it" (Proverbs 4:23). The condition of the believer's heart impacts everything they do. Those who are pure in heart are people who deliberately refrain from seeking after the greed, materialism, and self-centeredness of this world. These people are actively seeking the things of God and their lives reflect their attitudes. A leader with this kind of heart can have a profound impact. Every church, business, and organization needs at least one of these.

The Peacemakers

Peacemakers are often hard to find.

The biblical definition of a peacemaker comes from a beautiful Greek word that means "to bind or join together that which is broken or divided." In ancient Greece, a peacemaker was an emissary sent to beseech peace and was sometimes used to describe strong rulers who established harmony by force.

Jesus wasn't referring to people with peaceful dispositions; he was referring to people who actively intervene to bind together those that are divided. By making peace, kingdom citizens manifest themselves as children of God. To be called the "child of" gives an indication that the child behaves or looks like the parent. How much more of a compliment could anyone receive than one that says, "You look and behave like a child of God?"

This is the type of peace Jesus was describing when he said in John 4:27: "Peace I leave with you; My peace I give to you; not as the world gives, do I give to you. Let not your heart be troubled, nor let it be fearful." "Peacemaking" is what happened at the cross when sinners were reconciled to God (Romans 5:10-11). God and man were once again bound together in peace.

Those Who Are Righteous

Lastly, Jesus talked about those who live a righteous life. He stated that the Kingdom of God belongs to people like these. It is not by coincidence that Jesus placed this characteristic last. The righteousness that Jesus referred to is not self-righteousness. It is a characteristic that we receive when we are true followers of Christ. Righteousness is only gained through a committed relationship with the Heavenly Father.

The Sermon on the Mount shows the group dynamics that any team leader would be wise to look at carefully. Human characteristics are unique. Jesus' sermon to this crowd of people recognizes this quality.

The influence of Jesus has proven to proclaim a distinct message. When one examines His leadership style, it is obvious that He had a strategy to change and connect people. Jesus taught His disciples that the rulers of the world lord their authority over their subjects, but if His followers wished to become great they must become humble servants. Jesus had a plan to engage the heart with the mind as evidenced by His teachings from the Sermon on the Mount.

From the beginning of His ministry on earth, Jesus made it clear His plan was not to do everything on His own. The first action that Christ did after spending time in the wilderness prior to His ministry was to go on a recruiting crusade. This endeavor was to gather a group of men who had a desire to work together. This approach is shown in John's account of Jesus' first strategy development of leadership. The gospel of John says, "Now Jesus learned that the Pharisees had heard that he was gaining and baptizing more disciples than John—although in fact it was not Jesus who baptized, but his disciples" (John 4:1-2).

Early on, Jesus empowered others to do the work of the ministry. Chuck Colson, in his book, *The Body*, says that becoming a true servant leader calls for the believer to develop three characteristics. The first area of personal growth deals with reassessing one's personal objectives. Is our goal to serve self or is it to serve God? This first question must be clarified before growth as a servant will ever take place. Second, the goal of a healthy servant-leader should be to work hard to avoid every kind of temptations. Third, one who has a deep desire to follow Jesus will place himself or herself in the company of others who are trying to be obedient to the teaching and instruction of Christ.[4]

True servant-leadership has nothing to do with position or authority. Servant-leadership is not found by giving someone instructions—it is a change of heart. Servant-leadership involves recognizing one's dependence upon God and being keenly aware of sin. True servant-leaders have a gentle but controlled strength, drawing on the authority and power of God. They long for righteousness, are merciful to others, are pure inside and out, and seek to reconcile people to each other and God. This type of leader will naturally draw people to want to follow.

A strong servant-leader is not someone who has been given a position of power to lead others. The best definition of a servant-leader is *someone who gives of himself or herself and has followers!*

> The best definition of a servant-leader is *someone who gives of himself or herself and has followers!*

Discipleship: What Does This Mean?

But how do Christian leaders influence others to follow them as Christ did with His disciples? The answer is best understood by defining the word "disciple." A Christian is a follower or *disciple* of Jesus, someone who believes Jesus is the *Christ* or Messiah. A disciple refers to any "student," "pupil," "apprentice," or "adherent," as opposed to a "teacher." In the ancient world, however, the word "disciple" was most often associated with a devoted follower of a great religious leader or teacher of philosophy. In the Jewish world, a disciple was one who willingly submitted himself to a rabbi's authority. They surrendered to a particular rabbi's interpretive view of Scripture. This was a normal decision for observant Jewish young men.

In the same way, those who follow Jesus are His disciples. This is why Paul said, "Follow my example, as I follow the example of Christ" (1 Corinthians 11:1). Paul was continuing the commission Jesus left His followers with before ascending to heaven, to "go and make disciples of all nations" (Matthew 28:19).

Thus, true Christian servant-leaders are godly people with the character of Christ. And what was Jesus' character like? He was compassionate and loving, forgiving, gentle, prayerful, and patient. He exhibited self-control, and above all, was a humble servant.

Naturally, if Jesus' disciples were imitating Him, they too had these characteristics. They also had a clear understanding as to where they were headed. It can be easily said that a true follower of Jesus is a person who has character, vision, and influence. However, this influence will never be accomplished *without* character and vision. Those who walk with God and have character will have followers.[5]

When Jesus began His ministry in the first century, He began by recruiting students. These first followers were His twelve disciples. They were His students, voluntarily connecting themselves to Jesus with the goal of imitating Him as rabbi. The calling of these men showed a clear strategy. Jesus did not recruit His disciples out of the religious circles of His day; He recruited simple, common men. But His overall goal and purpose in doing so was big: to introduce the Kingdom of God to the world.

As Jesus began this process, He first acquainted Himself to some men who were brothers, Simon Peter, and Andrew. The next two men He brought into His ministry were James and John, who were also brothers. All four of these men were fishermen.

As Jesus familiarized Himself to these men, He made a very simple statement to them, "Come, follow me," Jesus said, "and I will send you out to fish for people" (Matthew 4:19). These brothers and friends became four of the strongest disciples Jesus had. Why is that true? It is because Jesus took the skills and talents that God had already gifted these men with and assured them they could use these skills for a greater cause.

At the very inception of His ministry, Jesus revealed that the character of a servant-leader empowers others to serve. This became the basis of His three-year ministry.

This recruitment technique is the foundational principle for the creation of strong servant-leadership. Jesus' goal was to take men who knew how to fish for a living and help them to use their "fishing" skills to introduce people to the Kingdom of God. Jesus unlocked the potential in each person while respecting their freedom to choose to respond. Jesus extended the invitation to Simon Peter, Andrew, James, and John, and they responded. Jesus also used his social influence to maximize the skills of Simon Peter, Andrew, James, and John toward the achievement of a unified goal.

At the very inception of His ministry, Jesus revealed that the character of a servant-leader empowers others to serve. This became the basis of His three-year ministry.

Christ Taught His Disciples Through His Actions

The verbal teachings of Jesus are very powerful. The words that Jesus spoke and the stories and parables He taught have no equal, and are lessons even known to the secular world. However, there are many non-verbal lessons people often ignore when it comes to the teachings of Christ. These teachings are not by His words, but rather by His actions. What Jesus *did* was as powerful as what He *said*.

Once, while in the temple area, the religious "leaders" engaged Jesus in a debate with the intention of trying to trap Him with His response about a woman who had been caught in the act of adultery.

> At dawn he appeared again in the temple courts, where all the people gathered around him, and he sat down to teach them. The teachers of the law and the Pharisees brought in a woman caught in adultery. They made her stand before the group and said to Jesus, "Teacher, this woman was caught in the act of adultery. In the Law Moses commanded us to stone such women. Now what do you say?" They were using this question as a trap, in order to have a basis for accusing him.
>
> But Jesus bent down and started to write on the ground with his finger. When they kept on questioning him, he straightened up and said to them, "Let any one

15

of you who is without sin be the first to throw a stone at her." Again he stooped down and wrote on the ground.

At this, those who heard began to go away one at a time, the older ones first, until only Jesus was left, with the woman still standing there. Jesus straightened up and asked her, "Woman, where are they? Has no one condemned you?"

"No one, sir," she said.

"Then neither do I condemn you," Jesus declared. "Go now and leave your life of sin." – John 8:2-11

Don't miss the invaluable lesson for servant-leaders in this one event. When the woman was brought to Jesus, His response was immediate, though at first He said nothing. He bent down on His knee and began to write something in the sand. He did not speak about the accusations that were made concerning this woman. What did the accusers see when Jesus bent down and began to write in the sand? Whatever He was writing caused the elders in the group to drop their rocks first and walk away from the woman they were accusing. Could He have been quietly giving these men time to think about their own mistakes and failures as He wrote in the sand?

An Action Plan to Train Others

Servant-leadership is not about teaching people through words alone. A true servant-leader focuses on one's actions, and the attitudes that fuel those actions. Jesus had a clear and direct strategy for his ministry. He not only taught in simple parables but also had a clear, straightforward plan for his disciples' actions.

> Servant-leadership is not about teaching people through words alone. A true servant-leader focuses on one's actions, and the attitudes that fuel those. actions.

In the gospel according to Luke, the author records the leadership styles and strategies of Jesus as it applies to His ministry. In his account of Christ's teachings, Luke points out Jesus' basic action strategies for his disciples as they go into various communities to teach about the kingdom of God.

> "After this the Lord appointed seventy-two others and sent them two by two ahead of him to every town and place where he was about to go. He told them, "The harvest is plentiful, but the workers are few. Ask the Lord of the harvest, therefore, to send out workers into his harvest field. Go! I am sending you out like lambs among wolves. Do not take a purse or bag or sandals; and do not greet anyone on the road.
>
> "When you enter a house, first say, 'Peace to this house.' If someone who promotes peace is there, your peace will rest on him or her; if not, it will return to you. Stay there, eating and drinking whatever they give you, for the worker deserves his wages. Do not move around from house to house.
>
> "When you enter a town and are welcomed, eat what is offered to you. Heal the sick that are there and tell them, 'The kingdom of God has come near to you.' But when you enter a town and are not welcomed, go into its streets and say, 'Even the dust of your town we wipe from our feet as a warning to you. Yet be sure of this: The kingdom of God has come near.' I tell you, it will be more bearable on that day for Sodom than for that town. – Luke 10:1-12

These strategies of Jesus helped to develop the servant-leadership style of each of His disciples by teaching them to:

- Enter into a new environment with a positive attitude
- Be thankful for what is offered to them by those they lead

- Make a commitment to those they are trying to teach
- Use their skills and gifts among people who welcome them
- Not waste their time or skills on those who are unwilling to learn

Often servant-leaders spend their time and energy trying to connect with those who do not want to join the work of the Kingdom. All servant-leaders have the ability to choose where they will spend their time. Investing energy in an environment that is not welcoming can be exhausting, but following Jesus' example in training willing followers can be extremely rewarding.

CHAPTER 2

The Building Blocks of Servant-Leadership

I have set you an example that you should do as I have done for you. Very truly I tell you, no servant is greater than his master, nor is a messenger greater than the one who sent him. Now that you know these things, you will be blessed if you do them. - John 13:15-17

What Jesus Taught About Servant-Leadership

The gospel of Mark begins by telling about the fundamental characteristics of Jesus as a servant-leader. When one reads the first chapter of Mark, there are some distinctive traits of Christ that are evident. The biblical truths of His teachings are valuable to anyone attempting to serve and lead.

Jesus Taught That Servant-Leaders Were Not Self-Promoting (Mark 1:11)

As Jesus began His ministry, He made it clear that there was a great power at work. He was/is that power! The fact that He placed Himself under John the Baptist's care to allow Himself to be baptized showed that Jesus was going to teach His followers that submission does not mean weakness. In fact, this was the first expression in His ministry of what true servant-leadership looks like to other people.

> The fact that He placed Himself under the care of John the Baptist to allow Himself to be baptized showed that Jesus was going to teach His followers that submission does not mean weakness.

In Matthew 3:13-15 the Bible explains in more detail why Jesus began His ministry by not promoting Himself, but instead allowing John to be in charge. Matthew writes these words:

> "Then Jesus came from Galilee to the Jordan to be baptized by John. But John tried to deter him, saying, "I need to be baptized by you, and do you come to me?" Jesus replied, "Let it be so now; it is proper for us to do this to fulfill all righteousness." Then John consented" (Matthew 3:13-15).

Jesus' first actions in public ministry were to set a firm foundation for the creation of what a true serving leader should look like.

Jesus Taught That Servant-Leaders Were Obedient to the Holy Spirit (Mark 1:12-13)

After Jesus was baptized, the gospel writer says, "at once the Spirit sent Him out into the wilderness, and he was in the wilderness forty days, being tempted by Satan. He was with the wild animals, and angels attended Him." Matthew tells this story of Jesus going into the wilderness in more detail.

> "Then Jesus was led by the Spirit into the wilderness to be tempted by the devil. After fasting forty days and forty nights, he was hungry. The tempter came to him and said, "If you are the Son of God, tell these stones to become bread."
>
> "Jesus answered, "It is written: 'Man shall not live on bread alone, but on every word that comes from the mouth of God."
>
> Then the devil took Jesus to the holy city and had Him stand on the highest point of the temple. "If you are the Son of God," he said, "throw yourself down. For it is written:
>
> "'He will command his angels concerning you, and they will lift you up in their hands, so that you will not strike your foot against a stone."
>
> Jesus answered him, "It is also written: 'Do not put the Lord your God to the test."
>
> Again, the devil took him to a very high mountain and showed him all the kingdoms of the world and their splendor. "All this I will give you," he said, "if you will bow down and worship me."

Jesus said to him, "Away from me, Satan! For it is written: 'Worship the Lord your God, and serve him only.'

Then the devil left him, and angels came and attended him." – Matthew 4:1-11

This intense period of temptation concluded with Jesus proclaiming the aim of His ministry is to serve God "and ***serve him only***" (Matthew 4:11b, emphasis added). Jesus was tested in every way known to man in these three temptations.

Interestingly, John the apostle breaks sin into three categories. He writes:

"Do not love the world or anything in the world. If anyone loves the world, love for the Father is not in them. For everything in the world—*the lust of the flesh, the lust of the eyes*, and *the pride of life*—comes not from the Father but from the world. The world and its desires pass away, but whoever does the will of God lives forever." – 1 John 2:15-17

All sins that hinder someone from being able to serve God fall into one of these three categories: *the lust of the flesh, the lust of the eyes*, and *the pride of life.*

Now, consider how Jesus' temptation and John's teachings go together:

> All sins that hinder someone from being able to serve God fall into one of these three categories, the lust of the flesh, the lust of the eyes, and the pride of life.

- *The lust of the flesh – "If you are the Son of God, tell these stones to become bread."*
- *The lust of the eyes – "Again, the devil took him to a very high mountain and showed him all the kingdoms of the world and their*

> splendor. '*All this I will give you*,' he said, '*if you will bow down and worship me.*'"
> • *The pride of life* – "*Then the devil took him to the holy city and had him stand on the highest point of the temple. 'If you are the Son of God,' he said, 'throw yourself down.'*"

Jesus had a choice when he was tempted; however, the purpose of His ministry was **not to be served,** but to fulfill the Father's plan for Him on earth. Like Jesus, we also have a choice when we are faced with temptations by sins of lust of the flesh, the lust of the eyes, or the pride of life.

Jesus Taught That a Servant-Leader Should Cast a Vision, with Clarity, Simplicity, and Directness (Mark 1:15)

One of the most dominant components of Jesus' ministry was His ability to be simple, clear, and direct. Not long after Jesus began His ministry, John the Baptist was arrested. When this happened, Scripture says, "Jesus came into Galilee, preaching the gospel of God, and saying, 'The time is fulfilled, and the kingdom of God is at hand; repent and believe in the gospel'" (Mark 1:14-15). Jesus didn't waste any time with fluff; he preached the gospel and exhorted His listeners to respond in repentance.

Jesus showed this same skill in His preaching and teaching. His ability to communicate an understandable truth through a simple parable was the foundation of all He did. When teaching about the Kingdom of God, Jesus told the parable of the mustard seed—the smallest seed in that area of Israel at the time. Everyone would have understood the concept of one small seed producing a great harvest.

Jesus taught His followers that their life mission was something that the Lord wanted each of them to discover. Those who have a clear vision have come to the point where they believe God has given them a life assignment. People who follow Jesus' teaching patterns will become great leaders who inspire and encourage others. They will help people become more than who they have been in the past. Those who follow Christ will become even more than they thought they could be. Great servant-leaders help people become something greater than themselves. Just like Jesus, great leaders will lead people to a better way of living.[6]

Jesus Taught That a Servant-Leader Is a Strategic Team Builder (Mark 1:17)

When Jesus called the first four disciples (who were fishermen) to follow Him, He said, "Come, follow me, and I will send you out to fish for people." When Jesus started the process of calling His disciples to follow Him, He began with men who had something in common. The act of Christ in recruiting the first disciples is a lesson in how important it is for any servant-leader to begin with people who share common traits and values. These four men did not have to explain themselves to one another, nor did they have to learn each other's backgrounds. They already knew each other and each other's skill sets.

Anytime a servant-leader is attempting to build a team, it is essential to have a core group of people who understand each other. This recruitment process establishes stability before diversity and conflict come along. Conflict will evolve in any group effort; but to reduce this possibility, servant-leaders should seek out like-minded followers. Jesus modeled this by recruiting disciples who created a strong and stable core.

> Anytime a servant-leader is attempting to build a team it is essential to have a core group of people who understand each other.

Servant leaders rely on persuasion and not positional authority when making decisions. Convincing others of the vision and purpose, rather than forcing compliance, builds consensus with groups. The result is a collaborative culture that communicates, "We are all in this together." In this environment, each person is committed to help others succeed. Individuals are encouraged to excel at their highest potential, and efficiency and effectiveness are the natural results. Jesus cast a clear and compelling vision: the Kingdom of God. He gathered a group of like-minded men, trained them up as disciples to emulate what He did so they could in turn disciple others, and released them to change the world.

Without a solid foundation rooted in the character of Christ, this type of leadership cannot be created. When a group sees the potential of what can be achieved when everyone works together for a common cause—God's Kingdom purposes—and when care and concern for individuals is fostered, the "mustard seed" will grow exponentially.

Jesus Taught That a Servant-Leader Is a Relationship Builder (Mark 1:19)

Jesus began recruiting His disciples by finding those who shared some common ground. This firm foundation led to His calling those of differing backgrounds. An example of this is relationship between Matthew the tax collector for Rome and Simon the Zealot (not Simon Peter). The make-up of these two individuals with completely different values shows how in Christ miracles can happen in relationships. Matthew worked for Rome by collecting taxes, while Simon the Zealot was an ardent Jewish nationalist. For Simon, the idea of paying taxes to Rome went against all he believed. It would not be out of line to say that Simon the Zealot hated Roman tax collectors with a passion. By bringing these two different men together, Jesus showed His power to unify people for a common cause. Jesus was all about building relationships, and it all started with a small group of twelve men.

What Jesus Modeled as a Servant-Leader

In the course of His ministry, Jesus modeled several crucial aspects of servant-leadership.

Jesus Expressed Control and Authority as a Servant-Leader When Needed (Mark 1:23-25)

Jesus possessed authority and often expressed firm control when needed. Once, when entering the temple area before the time of Passover, He found the area filled with moneychangers using the temple for illegal profit. In righteous anger, Scripture says he made a whip of cords and drove them all out declaring, "Take these out of here, and stop making my Father's house a marketplace" (John 2:13-17).

At the beginning of His ministry, Jesus encountered a man possessed by demons. Jesus expressed Himself in humility and humbleness while showing power and strength—modeling servant-leadership:

> "Just then a man in their synagogue who was possessed by an evil spirit cried out, "What do you want with us, Jesus of Nazareth? Have you come to destroy us? I know who you are—the Holy One of God!" When the demon made this statement, *Jesus said **sternly**, "Be quiet…*come out of him!" – Mark 1:23-25 (emphasis added)

There are times when the servant-leader will need to exercise firm authority. However, as Jesus demonstrated, this can still be done with the servant attitude of Christ.

Jesus Engaged Crises Head-on as a Servant-Leader (Mark 1:30-31)

A crisis will cripple many people. However, Jesus often engaged crises directly. The Bible says, "Simon's mother-in-law was in bed with a fever, and they immediately told Jesus about her. So he went to her, took her hand and helped her up. The fever left her and she began to wait on them" (Luke 4:38-39).

When Luke included this event in his gospel, he approached it from his occupation as a doctor. He noted that Peter's mother did not have just a fever, but it was "a high fever" (Luke 4:38). This type of illness was a very violent one that threatened possible death and was extremely dangerous to an old person. Jesus' approach was an expression of engaging the crisis directly. There will often be times when a strong servant-leader will have to take on what others fear, trusting in God for the strength to do what is being asked: "Be strong and courageous. Do not be afraid; do not be discouraged, for the LORD your God will be with you wherever you go" (Joshua 1:9). Jesus is the perfect example of a courageous servant-leader, in the face of crisis.

> There will often be times when a strong servant-leader will have to take on what others fear.

Jesus Was All About Empowering Others as a Servant-Leader (Mark 1:40-45)

As we read in the example above, Jesus' character as a servant-leader was all about revealing and releasing the best in people. Jesus' entire ministry focused on the empowerment of others. A perfect example of this was seen in the healing of a man with leprosy.

> "A man with leprosy came to him and begged him on his knees, "If you are willing, you can make me clean." Jesus was indignant. He reached out his hand and touched the man. "I am willing," he said. "Be clean!" Immediately the leprosy left him and he was cleansed" – Mark 1:40-42

The question was put to Jesus, "If you are willing, you can heal me." Jesus' response was quick and to the point. "I am willing!" This newly-healed man was now free to go and live his life—Jesus empowered him. Jesus' actions and teachings are reliable signs of what He thought was important in leadership, and these same things can equip any Christian to develop the skills of a servant leader.

CHAPTER 3

A Simple Strategy for Recruiting Servant-Leaders

He called a little child to him, and placed the child among them. And he said: "Truly I tell you, unless you change and become like little children, you will never enter the kingdom of heaven. Therefore, whoever takes the lowly position of this child is the greatest in the kingdom of heaven. - Matthew 18:2-4

Have you ever wondered why some organizations are successful, and some are failures? Many people think that the skills and talents of the leader are what make an active group healthy.

Who Are the Right People to Recruit?

There are those who believe that a casting of the vision and conveying the information to a panel of people will lead to success. There is a lot of truth to these statements; however, there is much more to the failures of organizations beyond the talents of one leader. It has a lot to do with the recruitment of those who are being led and leading these people.

Identifying the Right People

The reason that most organizations fail in developing healthy teamwork is due to having the wrong people in the wrong places. People tend to imitate those they respect. A person committed to Christ is not someone who says, "Do as I say, not as I do," but is someone whose actions speak loudly.[7]

> One of the first steps in developing servant-leadership is to have a healthy process of putting people in the right spot.

One of the first steps in developing servant-leadership is to have a healthy process of putting people in the right spot. The Apostle Paul understood this concept. Writing to the Ephesian church Paul said, "So Christ himself gave the apostles, the prophets, the evangelists, the pastors and teachers, to equip his people for works of service, so that the body of Christ may be built up until we all reach unity in the faith and in the knowledge of the Son of God and become mature, attaining to the whole measure of the fullness of Christ" (Ephesians 4:11-13).

This process is not a speedy one. Equipping the saints for service takes time, patience, and prayerful consideration, but the result, according to Paul, is unity in the faith, knowledge of the Son of God, and maturity.

Explain your vision so that potential leaders will clearly understand your goals and direction. This allows them to decide to either fully commit, or make a decision to invest their time elsewhere. Potential leaders come from different backgrounds, and may not fully comprehend your vision. If your vision isn't properly conveyed, potential leaders may not want to commit to it, and will likely experience frustration later when what they thought they were committing to ends up being vastly different. However, if you effectively explain your vision and provide clear direction, then those who do commit have been effectively equipped and you will have earned their respect.

Once potential leaders are identified and have committed, the next step is to connect them with the larger group of servant-leaders.

Connecting the Right People

Have you ever noticed that some people simply do not get along with each other? When developing a healthy group, the next goal should be to connect people into an environment in which all team members can encourage one another and effectively work together. When Jesus was recruiting His disciples, it was obvious that He was seeking out people who already possessed a little bit of character, a desire to see something new, and the willingness to influence their friends and family.

There are many ways for Christian leaders to do this today. One of the most powerful ways is through one-on-one communication. Communicating face-to-face is beneficial because it creates an opportunity to engage in uninterrupted conversation and you can really get to know someone better. By spending time communicating on a personal level, leaders can read a person's body language—nonverbal cues like gestures and facial expressions. They can listen and respond to concerns, and better develop the relationship. Though it can be time-consuming, this personal communication establishes a feeling of community. The leader is better able to socialize and interact with the other person. Bonds are formed, and a foundation for trust is created. This will ultimately impact the team the leader is trying to gather.

Get to know each person as a whole person. Make a point of doing something fun together. Visit their homes, get to know their family, understand their other life commitments, and genuinely express a desire to become their friend. But above all, listen. Invite them to share about their life, how they became a believer, what joys they have experienced, and what trials they have confronted. By spending one-on-one time with future leaders, the servant-leader will discover people's strengths and weaknesses and their hearts. Ask them "What is the *one thing* you just love to do?" What you want to know about a person as a leader will likely be revealed in these conversations, simply by asking the right questions.

At some point, there will be opportunities for group meetings and activities with potential and current leaders. However, when meeting with more than one person, it is always healthy to meet in a small gathering. Just as one has taken the time to get to know each person individually, everyone involved will get to know one another gradually in a way that builds trust and respect. In this manner, everyone will have the ability to engage in quality conversation without feeling left out. Though group meetings are effective, personal one-on-one conversation is best when trying to connect with others.

Once a leader has established a relationship with a new friend, it will be easy to see how he or she would add their unique strengths to a group. Ultimately, there will be bonds between one another so that the group can effectively serve Christ to further the Kingdom of God. God desires for all to work together. When servant-leaders take the time to build relationships, He will bless that effort.

After connecting leaders, the process of equipping servant leaders begins.

Equipping the Right People

When the right people are put in the right spot, equipping them to do the job well is the next step. One can never over train good people. In the book of Proverbs this advice is given, "For lack of guidance a nation falls, but victory is won through many advisers" (Proverbs 11:14).

A healthy servant-leader and a healthy team understand that learning is a lifelong process. Learning and growing never stops, it is always evolving. If the servant-leader has chosen the right people to join, they are not offended when more training or more equipping is suggested. In fact, Godly co-workers crave constant learning.

> A healthy servant-leader and a healthy team understand that learning is a lifelong process. It never stops for it is always evolving.

Thus, an effective servant-leader must be committed to equipping others. It is the only way to encourage personal growth. Those closest to the servant-leader will ultimately determine the level of their success. In addition, equipping others ensures the leader's success is lasting. There is no success without a successor.

Finally, equipping others is biblical. Paul writes that believers in Christ were given spiritual gifts for a specific purpose: "to equip his people for works of service, so that the body of Christ may be built up" (Ephesians 4:12).

Be aware that equipping others is not easy. It is tiresome and continual work that can sometimes be discouraging. Even the most wonderful, godly people will fail and disappoint. Commit to press on in spite of the difficulties, as Paul encourages his followers in 1 Corinthians 15:58: "Therefore, my dear brothers and sisters, stand firm. Let nothing move you. Always give yourselves fully to the work of the Lord, *because you know that your labor in the Lord is not in vain*" (emphasis added).

Hang on to the promise in God's Word: The Lord sees those who work for the Kingdom.

Empowering the Right People

Giving power to others is a healthy sign of intense servant-leader development and is one of the most effective tools any organization can utilize. Empowerment is supplying someone with power and authority, or with confidence and self-esteem. Through empowerment, the servant-leader acknowledges the talents and strengths of others, encouraging them in both action and personal growth. Underlying this is the concept that those the servant-leader is leading are not merely subordinates, but individuals in their own right. Servant-leaders provide direction when needed, but release those they are leading to fly on their own.

Empowering others is a biblical concept. Writing to young Timothy, Paul said, "And the things you have heard me say in the presence of many witnesses entrust to reliable people who will also be qualified to teach others." King Solomon wrote, "As iron sharpens iron, so one person sharpens another" (Proverbs 27:17). God reveals this plan of empowering others throughout the Word of God.

Teaching people to train others will help every member in a group find their skills and gifts. It will also mobilize and help them use the necessary resources to complete the task they have been asked to carry out.

A servant-leader empowers others to do the right things, at the right time. A servant-leader serves others and does everything in his or her power to help *them* achieve success, rather than being served for their own success. By giving up power of position and empowering others, leaders will gain the power of relationship and ultimately become more effective.

Along the equipping journey, the servant-leader must also be keenly aware of all human beings' need for encouragement.

Encouraging the Right People

Encouragement is all about healthy servant-leadership growth. It is not about dictating or suppressing the gifts of an individual. A good leader in any organization is attempting to find the skills of every group member and helping them become the very best they can become. A good servant-leader seeks the unique skills of every person on the team and encourages them to use and develop those skills. The Apostle Paul wrote this in his letter to the Church at Corinth:

> "Just as a body, though one, has many parts, but all its many parts form one body, so it is with Christ. For we were all baptized by one Spirit so as to form one body— whether Jews or Gentiles, slave or free—and we were all given the one Spirit to drink. Even so the body is not made up of one part but of many.
>
> Now if the foot should say, "Because I am not a hand, I do not belong to the body," it would not for that reason stop being part of the body. And if the ear should say, "Because I am not an eye, I do not belong to the body," it would not for that reason stop being part of the body. If the whole body were an eye, where would the sense of hearing be? If the whole body were an ear, where would the sense of smell be? But in fact God has placed the parts in the body, every one of them, just as he wanted them to be. If they were all one part, where would the body be? As it is, there are many parts, but one body.
>
> The eye cannot say to the hand, "I don't need you!" And the head cannot say to the feet, "I don't need you!" On the contrary, those parts of the body that seem to be weaker are indispensable, and the parts that we

think are less honorable we treat with special honor. And the parts that are unpresentable are treated with special modesty, while our presentable parts need no special treatment. But God has put the body together, giving greater honor to the parts that lacked it, so that there should be no division in the body, but that its parts should have equal concern for each other. If one part suffers, every part suffers with it; if one part is honored, every part rejoices with it. Now you are the body of Christ, and each one of you is a part of it." (1 Corinthians 12:12-27)

God gave us all different talents, skills, and abilities for a reason. He never intended for only a select few to be equipped to do the work. Learn to appreciate the gifts of others.

After identifying, connecting, equipping, empowering and encouraging leaders, there is one more step!

Repeating the Process

Healthy groups will need to repeat the following steps many times in the development of a servant-leader mentality:

- Identify the right people
- Connect the right people
- Equip the right people
- Empower the right people
- Encourage the right people
- Repeat this process

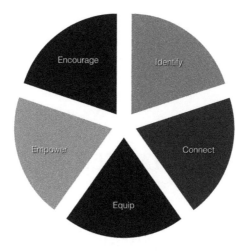

Though it initially takes time and effort, committing to this "cycle" will result in servant-leaders who are committed to their leader, the vision, and each other.

Recruiting and training servant-leaders for an organization is not impossible. Jesus' teachings revealed the greatest examples of how to lead people. His approach to leading His disciples is a perfect lesson in how to involve individuals in something greater than themselves. The way Jesus brought His disciples together is a strong example of someone who knows how to develop the skills and characteristics of people.

Strong servant-leaders understand the importance of utilizing the skills of those they lead. Although the mission may be somewhat different, the use of the talents of those who are being led is priceless for any task or goal.

> Strong servant-leaders understand the importance of utilizing the skills of those they lead.

Jesus was very clear about what the mission was to be. That mission was to reach people with the message of the Good News. This must be the mission of the followers of Christ if they hope to become servant-leaders.

CHAPTER 4

Three Fundamentals for Developing Servant-Leaders

Though I am free and belong to no one, I have made myself a slave to everyone, to win as many as possible.
- 1 Corinthians 9:19

Jesus' leadership style reveals some foundational skills for a leader to recruit other leaders. The first disciples that Jesus called to follow Him showed His apparent strategy to recruit and teach servant-leaders.

Every congregation needs the help of servant-leaders. What exactly is the act of such service? Serving others can be defined as helping others in small things, guarding the reputation of others, showing common courtesy, extending hospitality, listening, bearing the burdens of one another, and sharing the word of Life.[8]

Those are some great thoughts; however, the Bible is direct and clear as to what creates healthy servant-leaders. Both the Old Testament and the New Testament show the practices and wisdom of leadership examples. There are three fundamentals to servant-leadership development that can be found within the Bible.

An Attitude Adjustment

One of the first steps for servant-leadership development deals with the attitudes of the leader. The Old Testament book of Exodus tells a story in which Moses received advice from his father-in-law, Jethro, the priest of Midian, who encouraged Moses to adjust his approach to leading people.

God had identified Moses as the man who would lead His people out of Egypt to freedom. Moses would be the one who would take them to the "Promised Land." Initially, Moses took on a "lone ranger" strategy, a soloist approach. Among such a large group of Israelites there were naturally many disputes and questions of interpretation to settle. Apparently Moses was the only recognized judge in the nation, and the job of hearing each case occupied Moses from morning until evening. He was exhausted, and his leadership was certainly not effective.

Jethro noted this and asked Moses about it. Jethro had some advice for Moses. His advice is found in Exodus 18:

> The next day Moses took his seat to serve as judge for the people, and they stood around him from morning till evening. When his father-in-law saw all that Moses was doing for the people, he said, "What is this you are doing for the people? Why do you alone sit as judge, while all these people stand around you from morning till evening?"
>
> Moses answered him, "Because the people come to me to seek God's will. Whenever they have a dispute, it is brought to me, and I decide between the parties and inform them of God's decrees and instructions."
>
> Moses' father-in-law replied, "What you are doing is not good. You and these people who come to you will only wear yourselves out. The work is too heavy for you; you cannot handle it alone. Listen now to me and I will give you some advice, and may God be with you. You must be the people's representative before God and bring their disputes to him. Teach them his decrees and instructions, and show them the way they are to live and how they are to behave. But select capable men from all the people—men who fear God, trustworthy men who hate dishonest gain—and appoint them as officials over thousands, hundreds, fifties and tens. Have them serve as judges for the people at all times, but have them bring every difficult case to you; the simple cases they can decide themselves. That

What you are doing is not good. You and these people who come to you will only wear yourselves out. The work is too heavy for you; you cannot handle it alone.

will make your load lighter, because they will share it with you. If you do this and God so commands, you will be able to stand the strain, and all these people will go home satisfied." (Exodus 18:13-23)

Jethro keyed in to a major problem in Moses' leadership: Moses took on every issue himself; he did not trust others' leadership abilities. Moses needed an attitude adjustment.

A Christian leader's growth also may require a personal attitude adjustment. When a leader admits he or she cannot do it alone and acknowledges that there are those who have greater skills and abilities, there can be success. This admission and attitude adjustment is what Jethro was encouraging Moses to do. That is why a healthy church needs staff, deacons, trustees, and team leaders to help with the day-to-day activities of a local church.

Including Different People

The second fundamental in raising servant-leaders is including different people. Jesus modeled a strategy in servant-leadership development that should not be ignored. The way in which Jesus recruited His disciples is a perfect design for strategic leadership recruitment and development. The New Testament Gospel of Matthew gives this listing of the men Jesus recruited.

These are the names of the twelve apostles: first, Simon (who is called Peter) and his brother Andrew; James son of Zebedee, and his brother John; Philip and Bartholomew; Thomas and Matthew the tax collector; James son of Alphaeus, and Thaddaeus; Simon the Zealot and Judas Iscariot, who betrayed him. – Matthew 10:2-4

At first glance this does not appear to be a diverse group; however, a more careful study reveals Jesus had a strategic plan in recruiting men of different character. Notice the diversity between the fishermen, a tax collector, and a Zealot. Including diverse personalities was Jesus' plan and strategy. Jesus was showing in His recruitment plan the power of diversity when handled in the right way.

Including people with diverse backgrounds, skills, personalities, and passions produces a group of people who can change the world. In fact, in Jesus' case, it did!

Reliance on the Unifying Holy Spirit

The third fundamental, and a non-negotiable, is relying on the unifying Holy Spirit. One of the last instructions that Jesus gave His disciples is found in the last chapter of Matthew:

> "Then the eleven disciples went to Galilee, to the mountain where Jesus had told them to go. When they saw him, they worshiped him; but some doubted. Then Jesus came to them and said, "All authority in heaven and on earth has been given to me. Therefore go and make disciples of all nations, baptizing them in the name of the Father and of the Son and of the Holy Spirit, and teaching them to obey everything I have commanded you. And surely I am with you always, to the very end of the age." – Matthew 28:16-20

When a diverse group of people can see themselves as a unified force, it is like a human body that has all its parts working in harmony. Strong servant-leaders understand that there is no one in the group who is greater or lesser

> Strong servant-leaders understand that there is no one on the team that is greater or lesser than any other person.

than any other person. Without the skills of each person, the entire group will suffer. However, without the Holy Spirit, even the most powerful group of men and women in the world will not be able to move a tiny stone.

Jesus told his disciples that he would enable them with an "Advocate" to help them. This person would be someone they could count on. "But the Advocate, the Holy Spirit, whom the Father will send in my name, will teach you all things and will remind you of everything I have said to you" (John 14:26).

The Holy Spirit is very active in leadership recruitment! Jesus was clearly guided by the Holy Spirit, but look at what His disciple, Luke, wrote at the beginning of the book of Acts:

> In my former book, Theophilus, I wrote about all that Jesus began to do and to teach until the day he was taken up to heaven, *after giving instructions through the Holy Spirit* to the apostles he had chosen. – Acts 1:1-2 (emphasis added)

The presence of the Holy Spirit was also a qualifier for leadership when choosing seven leaders to care for widows (Acts 6:3-6). In Acts 13:2-5, the Holy Spirit guided the selection of Saul and Barnabas, two servant-leaders commissioned to preach the Gospel in Salamis. The Holy Spirit clearly chose and appointed leaders to shepherd the early church:

> "Keep watch over yourselves and all the flock of which the Holy Spirit has made you overseers. Be shepherds of the church of God, which he bought with his own blood." – Acts 20:28

Jesus set a clear precedent that continued on, in, and through the first disciples: invite the Holy Spirit to be involved in the leadership process.

These three basic fundamentals—attitude adjustment, including different people and relying on the unifying Holy Spirit—are foundational in being a true follower and servant-leader of Jesus.

CHAPTER 5

Strategy
Growing Servant-Leaders Like Jesus Did

For even the Son of Man did not come to be served, but to serve, and to give his life as a ransom for many. - Mark 10:45

The leadership of Jesus is unique to any other leadership style known to man. His strategy in training His disciples was laid out in such a way to spread the Gospel for all time. This message of Jesus transcends the barriers of culture, time, and history. Although the effects of Jesus' ministry are limitless, there is simplicity to his leading.

Four Phases of Ministry

Jesus' style can be seen in the process of involving His disciples in four phases of ministry. These phases are described by what Bill Hull calls (1) The "Come and See" Phase, (2) The "Follow Me" Phase, (3) The "Be with Me" Phase, and (4) The "Remain in Me" Phase. Hull's definition of ministry development are strongly based in Scripture and is indicative of Jesus' leadership style.[9]

Come and See•

> And they said to Him, "Rabbi (which translated means Teacher), where are you staying?" He said to them, "Come and you will see" (John 1:38-39).

In the first phases of His ministry, Jesus' invitation to His followers was for them to only "come and see" what was taking place. As Jesus began His public ministry, He began by giving this simple invitation to the disciples. "What do you seek?" And they said to Him, "Rabbi (which translated means Teacher), where are you staying?" He said to them, "Come and you will see" (John 1:38-39). There can be no doubt that the leadership style of Jesus was one that invoked curiosity. The increase of Jesus' followers took a natural turn when Andrew went to find his brother Simon (John 1:40). The invitation from Andrew to Simon was a "come and see" type suggestion. This process did not stop with the two brothers. The next disciple according to John's gospel was Phillip.

Phillip followed the pattern of Andrew. He found Nathanael and told him to come and see Jesus even after Nathanael criticized the fact that Jesus was from Nazareth (John 1:45-46). The beginning of Jesus' ministry did not start the disciples with teaching, preaching, or healing. It began by giving an introduction to "come and see". It is interesting how this invitation after being given by Jesus became part of His followers' behavior and conversation.

The Master Teacher taught his followers by setting the example and the standard for ministry. There can be no doubt that Jesus' strategy was effective. "People need to be convinced of the presence and power of God if they are to catch the vision of his kingdom on the earth."[10] It was the strategy of Jesus to have the disciples learn from Him by following, watching, and repeating His behavior.

Follow Me•

The next phase of His public ministry was an invitation to "follow." The concept of following calls for basic fundamental behaviors from the one asking others to support him. "Come, follow me," Jesus said, "and I will send you out to fish for people" (Matthew 4:19). The implication here is that Jesus can take skills already developed and teach someone how to use what they know for the Kingdom. There was not an attempt by Christ to turn His followers from all they knew, but rather to take what they knew and turn them into disciples for the Kingdom of God.

The leadership style of Christ is one that includes the visual senses (come and see). There is no doubt that following Christ and watching how He performed ministry was as much a teaching experience as His words. Jesus used the phrase "follow me" in every gospel (Matthew 4:19, 8:22, 9:9, 16:24, 19:21; Mark 1:17, 2:14, 8:34, 10:21; Luke 5:27, 9:23, 9:59,

> "Come, follow me," Jesus said, "and I will send you out to fish for people" (Matt. 4:19).

18:22; John 1:43, 10:27, 12:26, 21:19, 21:22). One of the basic teaching and leadership styles of Christ is that of setting examples for others to follow.

A major adjustment that some pastors and church leaders may face is in the transformation of their leadership style into servant-leadership model. Many congregations have adopted a secular approach to ministry development, but the examples Christ set are quite different from a business world approach. A congregation could greatly benefit from something as simple as changing the terminology used to define their ministry. For example, adjusting wording such as a "ministry" rather than a "committee" could help identify what Jesus asked His disciples to imitate when He invited them to "follow." The "follow me" phase of Christ is a core foundation of Jesus' ministry and servant-leadership style. The overall goal of a healthy servant-leader is to imitate and follow the example set by Christ.

Be With Me•

In the gospel of Mark Jesus shows another aspect of His servant-leadership style.

> "Jesus went up on a mountainside and called to him those he wanted, and they came to him. He appointed twelve that they might be with him and that he might send them out to preach." – Mark 3:13-14

Jesus mentored those He was leading (Mark 3:13-15), by leading with His disciples alongside Him. He brought them with Him as He ministered, prayed, healed, and wept. They watched, and they learned. The Scripture teaches that Jesus went up on a mountain and called to Himself those He wanted to follow Him. It is obvious that a lot of prayers had gone into Jesus' planning. The multitudes had become larger by the day, and the Lord set an example for the future church on how to develop a strategic ministry. At that point, the Lord called men who, for the most part, were willing to follow Him in life and death.

> At this point, the Lord was calling men who, for the most part, would be willing to follow Him in life and death.

There are many who have discussed and debated why Jesus chose only twelve disciples. Jesus' ability to understand the workings of education and crowd dynamics was evident in His selection of only twelve men. It is almost impossible to experience closeness with anyone when there are dozens of people present.

It is now commonly held that an average person retains only ten percent of what he is taught orally. If that person takes notes and is assisted by visual aids, the retention level is about fifty percent. If a person participates in doing a related activity, the retention level jumps to ninety percent. To become active in the vital areas of ministry, the disciples of Jesus would need actual practice.

But what does a person need to be ready to labor in ministry for Jesus? A believer needs to grow in his convictions, to undergo supervised training experiences with critique, and to be taught certain essential ministry skills. It would be three months before Jesus commissioned His disciples to actual laboring. But in the meantime, there was much work to be done.

The strategy of Jesus began with the "come and see phase" then a "follow me phase" which led to a more intimate "be with me phase." The "be with me" phase was a time when Jesus called His disciples to a higher level of commitment. Jesus' strategy was to create followers who would be able to lead the multitudes, rather than tend to the needs of a multitude of disciples, falling onto the shoulders of an individual.

Remain in Me•

It is evident in Jesus' strategy that He was seeking men who would continue developing others long after He ascended into heaven. Everything that Jesus did and said was a part of His pattern of growing the Kingdom of God; His followers were the strategy by which Jesus planned to change the world. Jesus did not approach the masses of people who were willing to listen to Him. He approached a handful of everyday people, fishermen, who wished to be a part of something bigger than themselves.

> Jesus' training to these first disciples was of acknowledging they had skills that could be used for a greater cause.

Jesus' training to these first disciples was of acknowledging they had skills that could be used for a greater cause. Christ never expressed that their talents could not be applied to this movement and He never intended to insult His followers in any way.

Christ came to give of Himself. This serving attitude was his strategy. The call for every Christian is to sacrifice, not only in service to Jesus and the Kingdom of God but also to mankind. The foundation of servant-leadership is to show the character of Jesus in one's behavior.

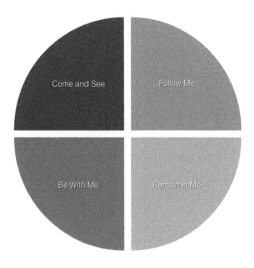

CHAPTER 6

Investing in Others
As A Servant-Leader Coach

*Jesus said to them, "The kings of the Gentiles lord it over them; and those who exercise authority over them call themselves Benefactors. But you are not to be like that. Instead, the greatest among you should be like the youngest, and the one who rules like the one who serves. –
Luke 22:25-26*

The business world has been discovering for the past few decades how important it is to invest in people personally and one-on-one. Studies have shown that training along with personal coaching produce far greater results than the training alone. Some companies discovered that when an individual was trained and then were assigned to a personal teacher, they were able to increase their commissions nearly 300 percent.[11]

The Servant Coaching Strategy of Jesus

John Mott, a Christian leader at the beginning of the twentieth century, is actually not known by many Christians. He was a Methodist layman who created the Christian Student Movement. During his lifetime, Mott was offered many prestigious leadership roles that he declined to accept. Some of these positions included an ambassadorship to China, president of Princeton University, and Secretary of State of the United States. Mott refused to take any of these positions due to his commitment to serve the Church of Jesus. Mott defined a servant-leader as "one who knows the road, who can keep ahead, and who can pull others after him."[12]

Mott's definition of a servant-leader is drawn right from Jesus' leadership. Jesus, too, had a clear and strategic plan in developing his ministry of servant-leadership. Jesus' daily practices would set the example for His disciples and future followers. First, Jesus made sure that He had time to be with the Heavenly Father before he did any leading, training, or teaching with His disciples (Mark 1:35; Luke 4:42). Second, Jesus had a consistent habit of praying for those He intended to lead. (John 17:6-19) Third, Jesus recruited a small group of leaders and invested in them. His goal was to share His vision and help develop their leadership skills (Matthew 4:18-22; Luke 5:1-10). Fourth, Jesus gave His disciples opportunities to

> Jesus had a consistent habit of praying for those he intended to lead.

fail and succeed. Fifth, Jesus created opportunities for His disciples to take full responsibility of His ministry.

Leading a group of people can be a challenging process. To get to the place where disciples take full responsibility for the ministry may need what is known as an active "coach." Many definitions can be found for the word "coach." Even though the word may have a modern use in the area of sports, this term also refers to someone who is a trainer, manager, teacher, tutor, or mentor. These words define Jesus. When the ministry of Jesus is studied, it is easy to find six basic instructions that he practiced in leading his disciples.

Jesus Was an Instructor

The first goal of any productive leader is to be sure that those they lead understand the direction and plan of the organization with clarity. Scripture says Jesus taught those who would later be His followers:

> "Jesus went throughout Galilee, teaching in their synagogues, proclaiming the good news of the kingdom, and healing every disease and sickness among the people." – Matthew 4:23

Jesus invited His disciples to come, watch, and learn from Him before He sent them out as His disciples. He was their instructor.

Jesus Was a Director

A director aims to supervise people without making members feel like secondary citizens. Proverbs 11:14 says, "For *lack of guidance* a nation falls, but victory is won through many advisers" (emphasis *added*). When Jesus called the fishermen, He told them that He wanted to make them "fishers of men." A servant-leader's overall goal is to guide others without coming across as degrading or insulting.

Jesus Was a Prompter

A prompter in the acting world is a person seated out of sight of the audience who supplies a forgotten word or line to an actor during the performance of a play. This behavior is what Jesus did when He recruited seventy-two disciples to go out two-by-two and share the Good News. Jesus did not go with the disciples, but like a good lead teacher, he stood by to help when He was needed. (Luke 10:1)

Once, when it was growing dark, Jesus' disciples came to Him and said, "This place is desolate and the hour is already late; so send the crowds away, that they may go into the villages and buy food for themselves" (Matthew 14:15). Jesus, tired from a long day's work, could have agreed and sent the crowds away. Instead, He prompted His disciples to address the problem themselves, by being part of the solution. He replied to the "They do not need to go away; you give them something to eat!" (Matthew 14:16).

By prompting the disciples to action to serve the masses of hungry people, Jesus was actually multiplying Himself. He was creating more servant-leaders.

Jesus Was a Tutor

A good servant-leader sees the value of the one person. A tutor is typically one who teaches a single student or a small group. A good coach sees the value in individuals. Jesus often taught large groups, such as the thousands who heard Jesus message on the hillside in Capernaum of the Sermon on the Mount. But The New Testament tells of several occasions when Jesus encountered His disciples and followers one-on-one.

Once a Pharisee named Nicodemus approached Jesus secretly at night. Nicodemus wanted to know how to enter the Kingdom of God, to which Jesus replied, "You must be "born again." Nicodemus was confused and asked, "How can this be?" (John 3:9). Jesus lovingly replied:

> "You are Israel's teacher," said Jesus, "and do you not understand these things? Very truly I tell you, we speak of what we know, and we testify to what we have seen, but still you people do not accept our testimony. I have spoken to you of earthly things and you do not believe; how then will you believe if I speak of heavenly things? No one has ever gone into heaven except the one who came from heaven—the Son of Man. Just as Moses lifted up the snake in the wilderness, so the Son of Man must be lifted up, that everyone who believes may have eternal life in him." – John 3:10-15

Jesus' willingness to engage in a simple conversation with Nicodemus likely changed the man's eternal destiny.

Jesus Was a Trainer

A servant-leader coach does not have a problem in "drilling" the team. Just like a personal trainer who presses in to improve an athlete's physical condition, Jesus did the same for people's spiritual condition.

Asking questions and seeking answers from each team member shows the caring character of the trainer. On one occasion, before His crucifixion, Jesus asked Simon Peter a very direct and simple question, "Who do you say that I am?" (Matthew 16:15)

In the same way, even after Simon Peter denied Him, Jesus continued to "train" Peter after His resurrection. Three times Jesus commanded Peter to watch after the flock Jesus was entrusting to him (John 21:15-17). Not only was this a beautiful picture of Jesus' love and forgiveness, it also is an example of Jesus as a trainer.

Jesus Was an Encourager

The overall goal of any servant-leader coach is to inspire those they lead. Encouragement is an absolute necessity for a successful team. Before his arrest, Jesus told His troubled disciples, "Do not let your hearts be troubled. You believe in God; believe also in me" (John 14:1). After Jesus' resurrection, and just before He ascended to the Father in heaven, Jesus again encouraged His disciples with the last words they would ever hear from Him:

> "And surely *I am with you always*, to the very end of the age." – Matthew 28:20b, (emphasis added)

Jesus knew the hearts of His disciples and that they needed encouragement to press on with the commission He had left them with.

These characteristics of a servant-leader will inevitably determine the direction and spiritual health of those who follow. A Christian leader or mentor is someone who is called by God to lead. They coach and lead others by their Christ-like character. A true servant-leader is a coach who demonstrates spiritual competencies and at the same time teaches other believers how to become a servant-leader.

Jesus taught his Disciples as a

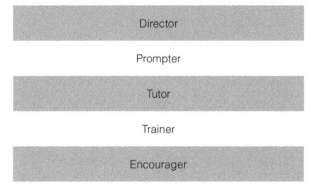

| Director |
| Prompter |
| Tutor |
| Trainer |
| Encourager |

These are five characteristics of a true servant leader.

CHAPTER 7

Why Servant-Leadership
Often Fails

No one can serve two masters. Either you will hate the one and love the other, or you will be devoted to the one and despise the other. – Matthew 6:24

Strong servant-leaders understand that the failures of those they lead should not be interpreted as negative experiences. They can use the failures of those they lead to help and encourage. Effective servant-leaders know how important it is to develop an environment where team members are allowed to fail and pick themselves up and move forward.

Peter, a trusted disciple of Jesus, discovered these statements to be true. Before Jesus was arrested, He told Peter that he would deny that he knew Him three times. Peter responded to Jesus in this way,

> But he replied, "Lord, I am ready to go with you to prison and to death." Jesus answered, "I tell you, Peter, before the rooster crows today, you will deny three times that you know me." – Luke 22:34-34

As the gospel story unfolds, Peter did just as Jesus predicted. Peter's bitter weeping was a sign of self-doubt, personal failure, and regret. Everyone has felt an experience of failure at some time or another just as Peter did. However, Peter's story does not end in his failure.

After the resurrection of Jesus, Peter took his stand in front of the people who had Jesus crucified. He preached a forceful sermon message about Jesus. As he concluded his message, he made this statement, "And everyone who calls on the name of the Lord will be saved" (Acts 2:21). After Peter had shared his message about Jesus with confidence and a sense of assurance, the Bible says that more than 3,000 people were added to the church in one day (Acts 2:41). Here is a man who denied he knew Jesus but was transformed into a powerful evangelical preacher who convinced thousands of their need for Christ. What does this story teach us?

- Strong servant-leadership can grow out of failure!
- Failure is not permanent.
- Anyone can recover after failure.

- Many great things can be accomplished when an individual is willing to pick himself or herself up from a fall when he or she is under the influence of the Holy Spirit.

There are those who are not prepared to do as Simon Peter did. Failure can be physically and emotionally taxing; however, that does not mean that it has to take control. Failure can be an influential teacher. Jesus encouraged His disciples not only in their successes but also in their failures.

Reasons Servant-Leadership Fails

Servant-leadership is one of many leadership styles, but is not accepted by everyone. Even in churches where the idea is embraced, some fellowships have a difficult time seeing it produce a healthy ministry. There are also many leaders who have tried the idea, but do not see good results. There are several reasons why some individuals and churches fail in understanding the use of servant-leadership.

It is not because the desire to grow as a strong leader is absent; rather, the desire needed to accomplish the task does not seem to exist. This behavior does not mean that the leader is weak; it only means that the skill to lead as a servant is not a dominant characteristic. What causes someone in a leadership role to fail at being a servant or to avoid the idea all together? There are five reasons why many leaders do not see the need in the development of their servant-leadership skills.

Micro-Management

Micro-managers believe they can do everyone's job better than anyone else. What is the result of this kind of leadership? Those who practice micromanaging will never see the full results of their servant-leadership potential. This type of behavior aims to manage with excessive control. Micromanaging suffocates the desire and vision of other people. This type of leadership is an insult to the character and skills of those being asked to accomplish a task. The reason that some organizations and congregations are unable to see their full potential is due to the stifling behavior of a micromanaging leader.

In contrast to micromanagers, servant-leaders empower equals. Effective servant-leaders recruit team members with gifts and abilities they don't have, and release those people to accomplish the goals that need to be reached however they see fit. That leader steps aside, and only connects back in to encourage.

The servant-leader recognizes their method of doing something is not the only method, or even the best method. Servant leaders allow others to excel as unique individuals.

Lack of Trust

Micromanaging behavior brings us to the next problem – a lack of trust in other people. If a leader has to have his or her hand on every activity of the organization, the potential for that group is minimized.

Do you think Jesus thought His disciples could do as good of a job as He was doing? Likely not! However, He knew His disciples had the capability to be world-changers. He had a firm reliance on their integrity, ability, and character. They were bumbling fisherman, tax collectors, and doctors. And Jesus was the King of the universe! But he trusted in those God entrusted to Him to do the job. He placed value in those He recruited. This trust undergirded the disciples, giving them the motivation take a step forward.

Likewise, it is important for servant-leaders to inspire trust in those they are leading based on the person's character and ability. This starts at the beginning, with building a strong personal relationship. When that relationship is solid, trust will be a natural by-product.

Self-Doubt

Some leaders suffer from their personal weaknesses. The self-doubt of a leader will not inspire followers. In fact, the self-doubt of a leader most often will cripple any organization. It is impossible to convince team members to believe in themselves if the leader suffers from self-doubt. The Bible gives some great advice about how to conquer self-doubt in Proverbs:

> "Trust in the Lord with all your heart and lean not on your own understanding; in all your ways submit to him, and he will make your paths straight." – Proverbs 3:5-6

Trusting in the mighty power of God can destroy self-doubt.

Resistance to Diversity

Diversity is a gift, not a threat! Even the business world realizes that diversity can bring about a competitive benefit. A leader who can recognize and encourage the various contributions of a person to a ministry or organization will lead it to a level of success and accomplishment that cannot be reached *without* diversity.

In his letter to the first century Christians, the Apostle Paul referred to the early church as "the body" of Christ. What was his point? His "point" was to assure the newborn Church that diversity could produce a powerful movement if those involved worked together.

Diversity is a gift from God and is an asset to any organization, business, or congregation. According to Paul, it is never to be feared. Clearly Jesus too foresaw the beauty of diversity within the church. Jesus quotes Isaiah when teaching in the temple in Mark 11:17 asking, "Is it not written, 'My house shall be called a house of prayer for all the nations?'" (See Isaiah 56:7). He also charges Christian believers to "go and make disciples of all nations" (Matthew 28:16-20).

Jesus constantly gathered leaders with different gifts, passions and backgrounds. God always intended the Body to be made up of diverse people (Revelation 7:9).

Fear of Uncertainty

Exodus, chapter 2, tells the story of how Moses witnessed an Egyptian beating a Hebrew. Moses went to the Hebrew's defense and killed the slave master. When Pharaoh heard of this he tried to find Moses to put him to death. Moses fled from Egypt and God challenged him to be the one chosen to deliver the Israelites to freedom. In spite of this Moses tried to back out of the job. He had a fear of what he couldn't comprehend. He told God, "Who am I, that I should go to Pharaoh and bring the Israelites out of Egypt?" (Exodus 3:11).

Uncertainty can destroy the work of any servant-leader, if those he or she is leading sense it. It is good for servant-leaders to remember this when leading, as a leader. It is also good for servant-leaders to be sensitive to those they are leading who may be in a place of fear.

Moses gave excuse after excuse as to why he believed he was the wrong man for the job. He cited his ability, his poor speech, and his lack of faith. But God accepted none of it and reminded Moses of one very important truth:

> "Who gave man his mouth? Who makes him deaf or mute? Who gives him sight or makes him blind? Is it not I, the LORD? Now go; *I will help you speak and will teach you what to say.*" – Exodus 4:11-12

When leading others who are fearful, effective servant-leaders remind those they are leading that *God is with them, and will direct their paths.* The prophet Isaiah understood this well, writing "In their hearts humans plan their course, but the LORD establishes their steps" (Isaiah 16:9).

When the Apostle Paul was writing his letter to the Church at Philippi he knew that he was about to be executed by the Roman government; nevertheless, he had some advice for the early Christians.

> "Do not be anxious about anything, but in every situation, by prayer and petition, with thanksgiving, present your requests to God. [7] And the peace of God, which transcends all understanding, will guard your hearts and your minds in Christ Jesus." – Philippians 4:6-7

Challenges will come about, failure will take place, and disappointments will happen. But servant-leaders must hold to a power and resource greater than themselves. And they must extend this same encouragement to those they are leading. The Apostle Paul chose Jesus to be his strength to overcome the fear of uncertainty.

Reasons Servant-Leadership Fails

Micro-management

Lack of Trust

Self-Doubt

Resistance to Diversity

Fear of Uncertainty

What Produces Fear of Being a Servant-Leader

Being a servant-leader is not always easy. Those who find themselves in the role of a servant-leader often find it overwhelming. For some people, the fear of being a leader carries with it some very strong feelings and emotions. Some leaders have never identified their anxieties of leading others. Fear is a reality. It also is something that has destroyed the servant-leadership influence of many great leaders.

Fear of leading can be approached in three ways. You can pretend that your concerns do not exist and hope they will go away; face your fears and try to overpower them; recognize your fears and claim them for what they are and deal with them by calling on the power of the Holy Spirit to help. The writer of Hebrews recorded a promise from God when he wrote, "Never will I leave you; never will I forsake you." (Hebrews 13:5b)

As you look at these three ways of approaching fear, recognize that the first two are weak. Ignoring a fear or trying to overpower it will only lead to exhaustion and burnout. However, recognizing concerns and acknowledging them for what they are, will allow any servant-leader to deal with fear in a productive way. Before leaders can deal with fear, they must recognize the areas of life that causes anxiety and fear. The following are fears that a good servant-leader might face.

Fear of Criticism

Most people do not want to be criticized. Sadly, leaders often fear the criticism of others, and when it does happen, they take it to heart. A very important principle to remember is that not all criticism is bad. Sometimes criticism is the very thing that will motivate a leader to change a bad habit, an ineffective way of leading or a character flaw.

But sometimes, criticism is just that…criticism. It stings, it may come from evil intent, and it may be intended to crush instead of build you up. Recall Paul's words to Timothy, a young Christian leader who was being bombarded with criticism and opposition toward the core of his beliefs:

> "Don't let anyone look down on you because you are
> young, but set an example for the believers in speech,
> in conduct, in love, in faith and in purity. Until I come,

devote yourself to the public reading of Scripture, to preaching and to teaching. Do not neglect your gift, which was given you through prophecy when the body of elders laid their hands on you.

Be diligent in these matters; give yourself wholly to them, so that everyone may see your progress. Watch your life and doctrine closely. Persevere in them, because if you do, you will save both yourself and your hearers." – 1 Timothy 4:12-15

Paul reminded Timothy to remain firm and steadfast in the character of God. He exhorted him to watch his character, life and doctrine closely. This would empower Timothy to withstand any criticism because no matter what was thrown his way, Timothy would remain pure before God. Like Timothy, servant-leaders today will receive negative criticism. Holding fast to the truth of the Word of God will enable the leader be able to remain standing.

Fear of Past Failings

There is one thing that makes a dream or a goal impossible to achieve: the fear of failing. Failure is what the strongest, most intelligent, most confident people fear. Whether it is starting a new project or succeeding at the old one, it's difficult to escape the concern in the back of one's mind that he or she might fail.

Being afraid to fail

- makes one fear what other people think
- makes one fear to pursue the future one desires
- makes one fear people will lose interest
- makes one fear and worry about how smart one is
- makes one fear disappointing people whose opinion one values.

These fears do not have to take place.

Fear of failure is actually rooted in a lack of belief. Recall the story of the twelve spies Moses sent to explore the land of Canaan. Ten of the twelve returned with a fearful report. Giants lived in the land! They could not possibly overcome them. This report in turn caused all of Israel to fear. The result was a forty-year stall; God had promised them they would take the land, but their lack of faith caused Israel's desert wandering.

The prophet Isaiah wrote, "If you do not stand firm in your faith, you will not stand at all" (Isaiah 7:9b) and the book of Hebrews promises the Lord will always be with his people (Hebrews 13:5). There is no reason to fear when God is on your side.

Fear of Making Mistakes

When one becomes afraid to launch forward because of fear, he or she misses many great opportunities. Jesus assured His disciples, as He was training them into servant-leadership, that they could be confident of His support for them. He allowed space for them to fail. During Jesus' last week on earth, they made mistake after mistake! When Jesus told them one among them would be a betrayer, they failed to understand what He meant even though He had been preparing them for His death for some time. "You do not realize now what I am doing, but later you will understand…. I am telling you now before it happens, so that when it does happen you will believe that I am who I am" (John 13:7, 19).

Servant-leaders will make mistakes. Making mistakes is simply part of living. Put mistakes behind you, receive God's forgiveness and acceptance, and heed Paul's words to "press on toward the goal to win the prize for which God has called me heavenward in Christ Jesus" (Philippians 3:14).

Fear of Leading

Are servant-leaders born? Do some people have the character of leadership from birth? Some folks believe that leaders are naturally born; however, Jesus taught His disciples how to become servant-leaders by His actions and teaching. Jesus taught His disciples in a way to dispel their fears. He said, "no longer call you servants, because a servant does not know his master's business. Instead, I have called you friends, for everything that I learned from my Father I have made known to you" (John 15:15).

Paul wrote to Timothy to encourage him not to be afraid to lead: "For God has not given us a spirit of fear, but of power and of love and of a sound mind" (2 Timothy 1:7).

Fear of the Unknown

Fearing one's limitations of knowledge has often held many potential leaders back from fulfilling their potential. Jesus addressed the fear of the unknown with His disciples prior to His crucifixion when he said, "Do not let your hearts be troubled. You believe in God; believe also in me" (John 14:1).

Fear of Being Rejected

The fear of rejection is a powerful and overwhelming fear! Often this is rooted in a person's upbringing or a previous rejection from a loved one or friend. Rejection can have a far-reaching impact into people's lives. Most people experience extreme nervousness when placing themselves in situations that could lead to being turned away. The fear of being rejected can become crippling; sometimes, a person may never try something new simply because they might be rejected for their attempt!

However, rejection is not always negative. In fact, Jesus warned about rejection in the Bible. In teaching His disciples how to deal with rejection, Jesus said, "If the world hates you, keep in mind that they hated me first (John 15:18). If Jesus who was sinless and perfect was rejected, His followers will be too.

What keeps someone from becoming a Servant-Leader?

Fear of Criticism
Fear of Failing
Fear of Mistakes
Fear of Leading
Fear of the Unknown
Fear of Rejection

Everyone will have to face fear at some time or another as servant-leaders. They will have to deal with it in some fashion if they intend to follow Jesus. The overriding goal of strong servant-leaders is never to be afraid of accomplishing the mission that God has called them to engage. This approach was definitely the strategy of Jesus in teaching His disciples about servant-leadership.

All those who attempt to follow Jesus and become servant-leaders will have to deal with failure and the fears it can produce. Here are some behaviors and practices that can help in dealing with the emotions and thoughts produced by failure and fear.

- Admit the mistake
- Accept responsibility
- Make restitution
- Reassess life vision and values
- Mourn your loss

- Move to closure
- Accept direction
- Establish new behavior and accountabilities[13]

Fear of failure is not something that any person desires. However, servant-leaders must be willing to fail if they expect to see positive results. Those who are not afraid to fail are people who understand the words of Jesus, "Do not let your hearts be troubled. You believe in God; believe also in me" (John 14:1). There is great strength in conquering all fears when one is a follower of Christ. Quite simply, do not be so afraid of failure. Of all God's prohibitions in the Bible, the Savior's word's "fear not" seems to stand out the most"[14]

CHAPTER 8

What Does a Humble Servant-Leader Look Like?

Be shepherds of God's flock that is under your care, watching over them—not because you must, but because you are willing, as God wants you to be; not pursuing dishonest gain, but eager to serve. – 1 Peter 5:2

When addressing the subject of humility and humble leadership, today's culture gives many varied definitions. When one speaks of exalting something that looks like weakness, most of the world does not understand the concept. Humility tends to be associated with weakness. But, according to author David Platt, "God actually delights in exalting our inability. He intentionally puts his people in situations where they come face to face with their need for him."[15]

This type of characteristic—a desperate need for God—is the foundation of true humility.

Humble Servant-Leaders Seek the Kingdom of God First

Jesus said, "But seek first his kingdom and his righteousness, and all these things will be given to you as well" (Matthew 6:33). His whole public ministry revolved around teaching His disciples the way of God's kingdom. When He exhorted His followers to "seek the Father's kingdom first" He was not using meaningless words. Jesus' whole life exhibited this command.

Jesus was a servant to His Father first, before He was Savior to the world. Because of this, He was able to serve those He came to save. This is an important principle for those who desire to lead like Jesus: service to others is nothing if it is not based on serving God first.

A man versed in the law once asked Jesus, "Which is the greatest commandment?" (Matthew 22:36).

Jesus responded with an answer the lawyer already knew: "To love the Lord with all of your heart, with all your soul and with all your mind. This is the first and greatest commandment" (Matthew 22:37-38). But then he added, "And the second is like it: You shall love your neighbor as yourself. In these rest all the law" (Matthew 22:39). Jesus was communicating to those who "had ears to hear" that kingdom life involves loving God first, and then others. Humble servant-leaders seek God's kingdom first, then seek to love and serve others. *This is Biblical servant leadership.*

When servant-leaders serve like Jesus, by seeking God's kingdom first and loving others, certain behaviors naturally result. Humble servant-leaders are more open and empathetic with those they lead and thus are better positioned to lead other people. They tend to be honest with those they lead and as a result are better liked and more efficient. Humble servant-leaders are willing to take a risk in others, as Jesus risked investing in the lives of common fisherman and selfish tax collectors. These types of servant-leaders know the "call of Jesus" is bigger and will last longer than they will; therefore, they gladly invest in others, knowing God is in the business of transformation. A true servant-leader has a goal of maturing new leaders.

Humble Servant-Leaders Gently Balance Forgiveness and Praise

Every position of servant-leadership provides a challenge, but a humble servant-leader has learned the balance between forgiveness and correction.

Everyone makes mistakes. In fact, people often learn more through their failures than through their successes. The humble servant-leader is quick to admit when he or she has done wrong and deals with the fall-out without placing blame on someone else. Those who attempt to grow as a servant-leader may experience disappointment, often at the expense of others' mistakes. A humble leader forgives easily by remembering how many times he or she has experienced forgiveness. Jesus taught this type of forgiveness when He taught His disciples how to pray, asking the Father to "...forgive us our debt, as we have also forgiven our debtors" (Matthew 6:12).

People like recognition for their accomplishments. A humble servant-leader is quick to divert attention to others and shares the praise for successes with those who may have had more to do with the success than the leader did. A humble servant-leader celebrates the success of others more than personal success.

A humble servant-leader is appreciative of the input of others. So much so, that this type of leader praises the actions of others far more than focusing on his or her personal accomplishments. Servant-leaders recognize that all good gifts come from above. The Bible teaches, "Every good and perfect gift is from above, coming down from the Father of the heavenly lights, who does not change like shifting shadows" (James 1:17).

No one can do everything. A humble leader can say, "I can't do that, or I'm not the one who should." Servant-leaders don't take all the key assignments for themselves but give out prime responsibility and authority to people he or she is leading.

This leader wants to learn from his or her mistakes and wants to improve continually. This type of servant seeks others' suggestions and feedback, not waiting until complaints come, but personally asking for the input.

Fundamental Behaviors of Humble Servant-Leaders

Many organizations, charity groups, and churches fail due to a lack of encouragement and instruction. Guidance comes from strong leaders. Humble servant-leaders have to decide how far they will go in inspiring those they serve to a higher level of ministry. Here are a few thoughts about the modest behavior of one who serves Jesus.

A Humble Servant-Leader Inspires Others

In the development of a ministry, the leader must have the ability to inspire those within the group. This act of inspiration creates in their minds a dream, a possibility, or a vision. This inspirational cheerleading mentally stimulates those within the team to envision and see the unseen. A good leader is a dreamer, and the ability to dream inspires others to see beyond themselves.

Humble Servant-Leaders Explain Themselves Well

A humble leader can create confidence in an organization of people and do it in such a way that people want to be a part of the leader's vision. A healthy leader can take the time to explain and lay out the details in a clear, concise fashion. This type of leader is never in a hurry. Jesus set the example by demonstrating through His parables and the Sermon on the Mount in Matthew chapter 5.

Explaining is one thing; articulating is another. Articulation is the ability to speak fluently and in a transparent fashion. A humble servant-leader is easily understood. There is no confusion with this person. There is no doubt in what the servant-leader has said. The explanations of a healthy leader are easy to understand. Jesus' practice of teaching through parables was simple, clear, and to the point. The Lord is not asking humble servant-leaders to be complicated, philosophical teachers. The best practice and sharing the message of faith is simply to follow the example of Jesus.

A Humble Servant-Leader Is Motivational

Motivation has a lot to do with the desires and ambitions of an individual or organization. Thus, it is difficult to accomplish anything without healthy motivation. There are times a person may have the desire to perform a task, but lacks the motivation to do it. A humble servant-leader recognizes this. To motivate a group of people will be very difficult if the leader cannot inspire, explain, and articulate the dreams and goals of the group. On many occasions when Jesus was trying to inspire His listeners He would start by saying, "The Kingdom of God is like...." A humble servant leader, a follower of Christ, will do their best when they follow the teachings of the Master.

CHAPTER 9

Living the Life of a Servant-Leader

Brothers and sisters, choose seven men from among you who are known to be full of the Spirit and wisdom. We will turn this responsibility over to them and will give our attention to prayer and the ministry of the word."

This proposal pleased the whole group. They chose Stephen, a man full of faith and of the Holy Spirit; also Philip, Procorus, Nicanor, Timon, Parmenas, and Nicolas from Antioch, a convert to Judaism. – Acts 6:3-5

Three Parts of a Servant-Leader's Life

In the process of becoming a healthy servant-leader, following the example of Jesus as a communicator cannot be ignored. Jesus had definite behaviors that He continuously performed before His followers. This behavior can be seen in three areas:

1) Jesus' public life
2) Jesus' personal life
3) Jesus' spiritual life

The growth of Jesus' earthly ministry focused on these three areas of communication.

The Public Life of the Servant-Leader

Public life is a part of everyday living where folks interact with people at work and in the community around them. The public sphere of a Christian is a social event of communication. Some people are drawn to large gatherings while others avoid them at all costs.

The words and actions of Christians will state what they believe in the public arena, whether they want to or not. You may not realize it, but others are watching what you say and do. On one occasion, Jesus asked His disciples, "Who do the crowds say I am?" (Luke 9:18). The disciples replied, "Some say John the Baptist; others say Elijah; and still others, that one of the prophets of long ago has come back to life." The disciples' statements prove that those who serve God are going to receive various opinions from different sources about their service to God. How one lives is the foundation for what he or she believes. Those who live their lives for the Lord, will be a light to those around them, whether they realize it or not.

"If we live, we live for the Lord; and if we die, we die for the Lord. So, whether we live or die, we belong to the Lord" (Romans 14:8).

The Personal Life of the Servant-Leader

Most people's personal life is somewhat guarded and the people they spend their time with is by choice. For the most part, this is made up of family and close friends and is usually a selective process. Jesus' personal life was no different. His personal life consisted of:

- His mother, Mary
- Peter, Andrew, James, and John
- The other eight disciples
- Mary, Martha, and their brother, Lazarus
- Many other unnamed disciples mentioned in the Gospel story like the seventy-two disciples Jesus sent out in Luke chapter 10.

Jesus ate dinner with these close friends (Matthew 9:10), stayed in their homes, wept with them, and celebrated with them at the yearly Feasts.

Jesus began His ministry by carefully selecting twelve men to become His disciples and developing a strong relationship with each. One particular close friend was Peter. During Jesus' life Peter was prominent, more often than not, because of his mistakes. Yet Jesus forgave him over and over.

In John 15:15, Jesus told His disciples He called them friends and not servants. There were some interesting criteria for Jesus when He chose His close friends. He prayed about the choice of his fellow servants. Jesus prayed all night before He chose the twelve closest people to Him (Luke 6:12-13). His choice of a fellow servant was not haphazard; the same should be said of any servant-leader. Jesus also made it clear that His friends lived lives of obedience to God.

"You are *my friends* if you do what I command." (John 15:14 emphasis added).

A strong servant-leader makes his closest friends those who follow the Lord. In order for His disciples to be able to share His strategy with the world, they had to know Him intimately; this was done by spending time with Jesus. A healthy servant-leader has this same relationship with the Savior; he lives a prayerful life, pursues obedience to Jesus' commands, and spends time with Him.

The Spiritual Life of the Servant-Leader

Another needed step of growing as a servant-leader is coming to a state of spiritual awareness. The Bible has some powerful passages of Scripture that teach about how we should think of ourselves. The Apostle Paul wrote to the Christians in his letter to the Church at Rome, "For by the grace given to me I say to everyone among you not to think of himself more highly than he ought to think, but to think with sober judgment, each according to the measure of faith that God has assigned." (Romans 12:3)

There are several times in Jesus' ministry where the Bible tells about Jesus leaving the disciples to get away. He often retreated from public speaking, from performing miracles, and teaching the disciples, to find respite in a quiet place. Jesus needed to be refreshed and rejuvenated, just as we do. Consider the following Scripture:

- Matthew 14:23 - After he had dismissed them, he went up on a mountainside by himself to pray. Later that night, he was there alone.
- Mark 1:35 - Very early in the morning, while it was still dark, Jesus got up, left the house and went off to a solitary place, where he prayed.
- Luke 4:42 - At daybreak, Jesus went out to a solitary place. The people were looking for him and when they came to where he was, they tried to keep him from leaving them.

- Luke 5:16 - But Jesus often withdrew to lonely places and prayed.
- Luke 6:12 - One of those days Jesus went out to a mountainside to pray, and spent the night praying to God.
- Luke 22:41 - He withdrew about a stone's throw beyond them, knelt down and prayed.

The servant-leader wisely carves out time to pull away from work, ministry, family, and friends to be alone with God. These three areas of Jesus', public, personal and private life are powerful lessons on how to balance life as a servant-leader. However, to fulfill these three areas of servanthood life there must also be conviction, commitment, and courage.

Three Attitudes of a Servant-Leader's Life

When anyone accepts the role of servant-leadership, his or her heart must be in it, for there is nothing weaker than being a half-hearted servant-leader. Servant-leaders understand there is a need to develop their role publicly, in a small group, and in the creation of a personal prayer life with God. They also understand that this calls for a conviction, commitment, and the courage to become a servant-leader.

Conviction

Many times servant-leaders come to the conclusion that for success to take place shortcuts must be made. Therefore, they are often tempted to compromise with evil forces to reach their goals. In many cases, servant-leaders become tolerant or they reach a place when they will do something they once considered wrong. But Jesus set the example in His temptation. As he began His ministry as a servant-leader, He was tempted in the wilderness (Matthew 4:1-11). To have conviction, however, means you refuse to conform to the ways of the world, even if the process of completing your goals takes longer, people become offended, or you have to give something up. Stand firm for what you believe, as Jesus did!

Commitment

Commitment to any effort will determine its success or failure. Commitment is a challenge. It will often call servant-leaders to stand-alone. Commitment is not always easy. Many followers of Christ have a commitment of convenience. They will stay faithful as long as it's safe and does not involve risk, rejection, or criticism. Instead of standing alone in the face of challenge or temptation, they check to see which way their friends are going." This type of commitment is weak.

Courage

Conviction and commitment, if practiced, will call for courage. This characteristic can often be intimidating and frightening. Anyone who possesses real courage will find that it is often a challenge that takes on many forms. Before His crucifixion, Jesus Christ challenged his disciples to be brave (John 14:1-4). God commanded Joshua to "Be strong and courageous. Do not be afraid; do not be discouraged, for the LORD your God will be with you wherever you go" (Joshua 1:9) before entering the Promised Land. God knew once they were in the land they would have many battles to face.

There will be many occasions when fear, anxiety, and intimidation attempt to dominate the mind of all those who are trying to be a servant-leader of Jesus. They will, as Joshua did, have "battles" to fight. However, courageous servant-leaders are confident. Gene Wood and Daniel Harkavy believe that "people who don't believe they can change their current reality will be pessimistic. Pessimism inspires no one. Optimism is the attitude that we are doing the right things, we are the right people, and we are in the right place. Not let's make a difference in our world. This attitude is contagious"[16] Convictions, commitment, and courage! These three words are great building blocks that every servant-leader will need.

3 Attitudes of a Servant Leader's Life

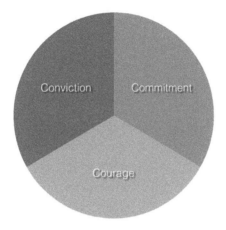

CHAPTER 10

How Do Churches Develop Servant-Leaders?

I have set you an example that you should do as I have done for you. – John 13:15

We often refer to someone as a "leader" only to discover that this is a title and not necessarily the exact characteristic of the person. Servant-leadership is more than a title or position. A true servant-leader is someone who has a calling, godly character and commitment. A servant-leader succeeds if his or her followers succeed. So the big question is, *how do churches develop people who become servant-leaders?*

The church must approach the topic of servant-leadership within the context of biblical doctrine. Otherwise, if leadership is formed from a secular, worldly foundation, leaders will not bear the character and thumbprint of Christ. Programs must be formed through the filter of enabling people to grow a Christ-like servant heart. The goal must always be growing people into their full potential as a multiplied servant-leader. Churches should strive to develop strategies and tools that are consistent with Jesus' character as a servant-leader.

The Call of the Servant-Leader

Placing someone in a position does not make him or her a servant-leader. Just because a person seems like "they might fit" can have detrimental, and sometimes damaging results. Just because a person is gifted in making a lot of money, does not mean that they are the best person to lead the stewardship ministry of a church. A person may be capable of giving a great speech, but that does not mean they are the right person to teach an adult Bible study. Servant-leadership is not about executing a program or effectively running an organization. Those called to be servant-leaders do not focus on themselves. Servant leaders have a longing to see others do well. Jesus told his disciples, "Give to everyone who asks you, and if anyone takes what belongs to you, do not demand it back. [31] Do to others as you would have them do to you" (Luke 6:30-31).

The Competencies of a Servant-Leader

Do you believe that God created this world, this universe, and even human beings? Do you think that God can put the right people in the right place at the right time? If you answered yes to both of these questions, then why stress so much about the *work* of the Kingdom of God? It is not God's design or plan for us to fail.

> "For I know the plans I have for you," declares the Lord,
> "plans to prosper you and not to harm you, plans to give
> you hope and a future." – Jeremiah 29:11

Think about your call, your character, and your competencies and let God use you as a leader. Your ability has nothing to do with whether God's plan will come to pass. But your refusal may cause you to miss the most exciting thing you will ever do while living on this earth!

Affirmation of Leadership is the Key to Success

In an article of *Our Daily Bread*, Marvin Williams noted that affirming leadership is the key to success in any organization. He wrote, "During a recent study, 200,000 employees were interviewed to discover the missing ingredient in their productivity…This research implies that receiving affirmation is a basic human need."[17]

When a leader encourages another person, the God-given skills and talents of those individuals are pulled to the forefront. The opposite takes place when a person is discouraged or criticized. Encouraging those who are being trained is like planting a seed into the soil. Poor soil equals weak growth. Rich soil produces abundant growth. Affirming actions (good soil) will produce healthy leaders (growth).

When servant-leaders practice affirmation through positive statements, kind words, and even rewards, they go beyond the present and create future possibilities. The words they choose to use play a productive or destructive role. Supporting someone with the right words in a helpful manner is an extremely healthy action. Here are some additional benefits to affirming others:

- Affirmation can help destroy stress within any organization
- Affirmation can help to produce healthy brain activity
- Affirmation can help in battling mild depression
- Affirmation can help to counteract negative perceptions

In 1 Peter 2, the author of the epistle affirms the early believers by telling them that they are: a chosen race, a royal priesthood, and a holy nation (1 Peter 2:9). The more people are affirmed, the more success a congregation will experience.

Servant-leaders who positively encourage others will grow strong leaders. One of the worst mistakes anyone can make in the development of future leaders is to use a negative approach. Jesus was always positive towards His followers. Notice His words of comfort: "Come to me, all who labor and are heavy laden, and I will give you rest. Take my yoke upon you, and learn from me, for I am gentle and lowly in heart, and you will find rest for your souls" (Matthew 11:28-29).

Influencing leaders to encourage others, especially those they are training, can never be under-estimated. What a person thinks of himself or herself can be healthy or destructive. Affirming the good and valuable qualities in another can breathe life into a person who is in the pits. Affirming those we are training to be leaders will help form an attitude of success in people (or organizations). There is no doubt encouraging leaders is a key to success!

The greatest example of an inclusive and affirming nature is found in the story of the prodigal son. In this story a son leaves his father and his family to indulge in a life of filth and sin. When the son returns home, the father welcomes him with open arms, no questions asked. The story provides a biblical example of one who was willing to forgive and embrace his "prodigal son" (Luke 15:11-32).

One of the basic foundational building blocks for any successful servant-leader is to follow the example and behavior of a loving and forgiving father. In the story of the prodigal son, this "father" is God. In spite of our sin, weaknesses, pride, and imperfections, God always affirms, forgives, and reminds us of who we are in Him.

Perfection is rare in this world, and sin is abundant. But those who follow the teachings of Jesus will be those who are also willing to forgive and love, even the unlovely. Those will be the world-changers. Those are true servant-leaders.

CHAPTER 11

The Praying Skills of
Servant-Leaders

One day Jesus was praying in a certain place. When he finished, one of his disciples said to him, "Lord, teach us to pray, just as John taught his disciples." – Luke 11:1

While reading through *Spiritual Leadership*, a book by Henry and Richard Blackaby, I came across this question, "Why should leaders pray?" This made me consider whether servant-leaders should be involved in regular prayer. Both Henry and Richard Blackaby believe that prayer is an essential leadership activity. It clarifies God's wisdom, it accesses God's power, it relieves stress, and it reveals God's agenda.[18]

Prayer and Servant-Leadership Skills

There are many opinions about how a group or congregation can best succeed. Strategies, planning, and vision-casting are crucial, but what about the roles that prayer and servant-leadership play in supporting one another?

Undoubtedly, prayer creates a healthy organization. The prayer life of any servant-leader, ideally, will focus on the lives of those they lead. If this occurs, it is the best guard against self-centeredness. In addition to guarding against self-centeredness, developing an intercessory prayer life for others is one of the strongest ways Christians can show their love for those they lead.

A growing servant-leader is a praying person.

Prayer With a Purpose

Gary Collins asks a very interesting question of Christians. "Have you ever noticed how easy it is to plan first and pray later? Or we don't pray until we get stuck and need to be rescued."[19]

Many people see prayer as one more practice to complicate their lives. However, a single request before God has more power in it than any fine lecture or debate. Real and commanding prayer does not need to take hours, but it does call for honesty. An authentic prayer life calls the Christian servant-leader to

> Real and commanding prayer does not need to take hours, but it does call for honesty.

present to God their needs with a sincere heart. Prayer is not about length and style as much as it is about honest connection with the Creator of the universe. In the 1851 Baptist Psalmody: Selection of Hymns by Basil Manly, these words were written in a hymn about prayer –

Prayer is the breath of God in man,
Returning whence it came;
Love is the sacred fire within,
And prayer the rising flame.
It gives the burdened spirit ease,
And soothes the troubled breast;
Yields comfort to the mourners here,
And to the weary rest.
When God inclines the heart to pray,
He hath an ear to hear;
To him there's music in the groan,
And beauty in a tear.
The humble suppliant cannot fail
To have his wants supplied,
Sin He for sinners intercedes
Who once for sinners dies.[20]

Praying With Goals in Mind

Why should servant-leaders in a church be actively praying with set goals? First, to be involved in prayer is simply following the example set by Jesus to do so. Prayer should be an active part of every church simply because Jesus set the example of an active prayer life. Thom Rainer writes, "Prayer is the power behind the principles. There simply is no more important principle in church growth than prayer."[21]

> "Prayer is the power behind the principles. There simply is no more important principle in church growth than prayer."

American college basketball coach, John Wooden, also had this to say about prayer, "Don't pray to win. Such a request is not biblical. Instead, be a winner by being honorable and staying satisfied with asking for the fullness of God's blessing, presence, influence and protection – for His glory, not yours."[22]

Prayer Taught By Jesus

Jesus' disciples approached Him with a request; they wanted to be taught how to pray (Luke 11:1). The following passage of Scripture from the gospel of Luke tells of that event.

> One day Jesus was praying in a certain place. When he finished, one of his disciples said to him, "Lord, teach us to pray, just as John taught his disciples." He said to them, "When you pray, say:
> "Father, hallowed be your name, your kingdom come.
> Give us each day our daily bread.
> Forgive us our sins, for we also forgive everyone who sins against us.
> And lead us not into temptation."
> Then Jesus said to them, "Suppose you have a friend, and you go to him at midnight and say, 'Friend, lend me three loaves of bread; a friend of mine on a journey has come to me, and I have no food to offer him.' And suppose the one inside answers, 'Don't bother me. The door is already locked, and my children and I are in bed. I can't get up and give you anything.' I tell you, even though he will not get up and give you the bread because of friendship, yet because of your shameless audacity he will surely get up and give you as much as you need. "So I say to you: Ask and it will be given to

you; seek and you will find; knock and the door will be opened to you. For everyone who asks receives; the one who seeks finds; and to the one who knocks, the door will be opened." (Luke 11:1-16)

The Lord's Prayer is the best guidance and instruction ever given on how to utilize prayer. It is a practice of 1) Honoring and believing in God, 2) Asking for God's provisions for taking care of one's needs, 3) Seeking forgiveness while practicing forgiving others and 4) Seeking protection from sinful behavior.

In addition to revealing to servant-leaders how to pray, the Lord's Prayer instructs believers in what *not* to do.

> "And when you pray, do not be like the hypocrites, for they love to pray standing in the synagogues and on the street corners to be seen by others. Truly I tell you, they have received their reward in full. But when you pray, go into your room, close the door and pray to your Father, who is unseen. Then your Father, who sees what is done in secret, will reward you. And when you pray, do not keep on babbling like pagans, for they think they will be heard because of their many words." – Matthew 6:5-7

Jesus instructs His followers to pray authentically. Don't put on a show or an act, and do not pretend. He knows everything stirring around in your heart and mind already. Babbling on just to be seen by others as "prayerful" or "godly" is nothing more than hypocrisy to God.

Instead, the servant-leader should pray both privately and with others. Christians can pray anytime and anywhere. Many people pray in a room in their home, such as a bedroom or office. Others might pray when they walk the dog, or when they are driving to school or work!

Prayer does not have to be out loud; the prayer of the servant-leader that is quiet is just as powerful.

Prayer is a healthy and powerful tool for all leaders. Jesus taught His disciples not only how to pray with His teaching but by His actions. Jesus prayed every day. Here are some examples of his daily practice.

- "Very early in the morning, while it was still dark, Jesus got up, left the house and went off to a solitary place, where he prayed." (Mark 1:35)
- "After he had dismissed them, he went up on a mountainside by himself to pray." – Matthew 14:23
- "Then Jesus went with his disciples to a place called Gethsemane, and he said to them, 'Sit here while I go over there and pray.'" – Matthew 26:36
- "Very early in the morning, while it was still dark, Jesus got up, left the house and went off to a solitary place, where he prayed." – Mark 1:35
- "But Jesus often withdrew to lonely places and prayed." – Luke 5:16
- "One of those days Jesus went out to a mountainside to pray, and spent the night praying to God." – Luke 6:12
- "Then Jesus told his disciples a parable to show them that they should always pray and not give up." – Luke 18:1

Servant-leadership is powerless without an active prayer life. Any Believers desiring to follow Christ must engage in an active life of talking with the heavenly Father.

CHAPTER 12

Servant-Leaders Create Change

Then Jesus came to them and said, "All authority in heaven and on earth has been given to me. Therefore go and make disciples of all nations, baptizing them in the name of the Father and of the Son and of the Holy Spirit, and teaching them to obey everything I have commanded you. And surely I am with you always, to the very end of the age. – Matthew 28:18-20

The focus of this book has been to help explain how Jesus defined service and leadership. The overall goal has been to show how these two actions work together. To become a servant-leader there must be a merging of "strong leadership with the quality of a servant's heart."[23] To appreciate that these two words are not in contradiction with each other one must first have a clear understanding of the characteristics of a faithful servant. Consider the following verses from the book of Matthew:

> Jesus called them together and said, "You know that the rulers of the Gentiles lord it over them, and their high officials exercise authority over them. Not so with you. Instead, whoever wants to become great among you must be your servant, and whoever wants to be first must be your slave— just as the Son of Man did not come to be served, but to serve, and to give his life as a ransom for many." – Matthew 20:25-28

Those who follow Jesus' teachings have distinct characteristics in the way they behave. Because of these characteristics they have a personal behavior that invests in people around them. They are not self-centered people. These types of believers are also those who demonstrate a willingness to help others. They remember the words of Jesus when He said, "Greater love has no one than this: to lay down one's life for one's friends" (John 15:13). Leaders who are willing to embrace the challenges of change must have a lower than average need for affirmation; a high level of curiosity and a healthy attitude of not allowing failures to bring them down.[24]

Those who have accepted the invitation of Christ to follow His teachings are also those who are willing to encourage the personal

> Servant-leaders are not self-serving. They invest themselves in the constant development of others.

growth of those people under their influence. These types of leaders are not self-centered and because of the influence of the Holy Spirit they have the ability to focus on the needs of others. They invest themselves in the constant development of others.

The call for every Christian is to give of themselves in service to Jesus and the Kingdom of God, and to their fellow man, including those inside and outside the church. According to the teaching of Jesus, it is not impossible to be a leader and a servant at the same time. Even after reading this book, it may still seem that these two words are in opposition to one another. Not so with Jesus. The bottom line of being a Christian and a servant-leader is to show the character of Jesus in our daily behavior.

How can the average Christian become a servant-leader that imitates Jesus? For this to happen it must begin with those who are willing to set an example. And those folks with willing hearts to lead are desperately needed! Without leaders, followers will disappear.

A church without servant-leaders can never expect their congregation to catch the fire of the Holy Spirit and the teachings of Jesus. Servant-leadership is the type of leading that will help create enthusiasm and dreams in a church of believers. Those who see beyond themselves have had their eyes opened to a bright future. These are the kinds of people who can create enthusiasm because they see a future that is being created by the example that Jesus set.

When a Christian agrees to become a servant-leader, like Jesus, they help to create a learning environment among other believers. One fact can never be forgotten: humility is the key! Servant-leaders must be willing to humbly admit that they do not have all the answers. This type of attitude will help create an environment that will draw many people.

An environment of real servant-leaders helps to cultivate a learning desire in all church members. When those who work within a congregation of people recognize that other people are the greatest resources the church has, servant-leadership will grow naturally. This type of attitude will cause people to listen to and take the time to teach one another.

It Is All About Grace

Servant-leadership, designed by Jesus, is the perfect example of grace. If a congregation of believers follows this expression of faith it will destroy practices of Christians being too hard on each other, and the conflicts that evolve and destroy many congregations will be overpowered. This will change the environment of the average church. Any congregation that has a desire to grow and flourish should base all they do on the most powerful expression of grace known to man. True servant-leaders, faithful followers of Jesus, approach their world in a spirit of grace that has room for failures. This does not mean that the church should be accepting of sick or habitual sins; however, it does mean that the overall goal of any servant-leader is to follow the teaching of the Master.

Peter had some advice for the early church in his first epistle pertaining to servant-leadership. His words can be a solid foundation for everyone who is trying to follow the example of Jesus.

> Each of you should use whatever gift you have received to serve others, as faithful stewards of God's grace in its various forms. If anyone speaks, they should do so as one who speaks the very words of God. If anyone serves, they should do so with the strength God provides, so that in all things God may be praised through Jesus Christ. To him be the glory and the power for ever and ever. Amen. – 1 Peter 4:10-11

The strategy of Jesus was a simple, yet powerful plan. He showed His disciples and followers that a true servant-leader is someone who invests himself or herself into those who follow. They also have a character that demonstrates a willingness to give of themselves to help others. This plan encourages the personal growth of those who are being led over the personal desires or self-interest. Jesus set an example of giving of Himself that was for the constant development of others.

The character of a true servant-leader is not fake or misleading. True servant-leaders do not try and create other leaders who are fake. They pursue creating leaders who lead by doing what the Lord created them to do. When we use our unique personalities under the leadership of the Holy Spirit, we become a powerful and useful tool in the hands of God.

Endnotes

Introduction

[1] *Christian Coaching*, Gary R Collins, NavPress, Pages 34-35
[2] *Discipled Warriors*, Chuck Lawless, Kregel Publications, 2002, p.112.
[3] *The 12 Essential of Godly Success*, Tommy Nelson, Broadman & Holman Publishers, Nashville, p.89

Chapter 1

[4] *The Body*, Charles Colson, Word Publishing, Dallas, 1977, pp. 303-306
[5] *Planting Growing Churches*, Aubrey Malphurs, Baker Book House, Grand Rapids, 1997, p. 99
[6] *Practicing Greatness*, Reggie McNeal, Jossey-Bass, San Francisco, 2006, p. 4

Chapter 3

[7] *The Power of Team Leadership*, George Barna, Waterbrook Press, Colorado Springs, 2001, p. 95

Chapter 4

[8] *Celebration of Discipline*, Richard Foster, HarperSan Francisco, New York, NY, 1998, pages 135-139

Chapter 5

[9] Bill Hull, <u>New Century Disciplemaking</u>, Fleming, H. Revell; Grand Rapids, 1984, p. 5
[10] Bill Hull, <u>New Century Disciplemaking</u>, p.25

Chapter 6

[11] *Leadership Coaching*, Tony Stoltzfus, Virginia Beach, 2005, p.38

[12] *Dying for Change*, Leith Anderson, Bethany House Publishers, Minneapolis, MN, 1990, p. 187

Chapter 7

[13] *Practicing Greatness*, Reggie McNeal, Jossey-Bass, San Francisco, 2006, pp. 76-80
[14] *Planting Growing Churches*, Aubrey Mapphurs, Baker Book House, Grand Rapids, 1997, p.70

Chapter 8

[15] *Radical*, David Platt, Multnomah Books, Colorado Springs, 2010, p. 47

Chapter 9

[16] *Leading Turnaround Teams*, Gene Wood and Daniel Harkavy, Church Smart Resources, St. Charles, IL, 2004, p.51

Chapter 10

[17] Marvin Williams, Our Daily Bread, September 10, 2013

Chapter 11

[18] Blackaby, *Spiritual Leadership*, p.153
[19] *Christian Coaching*, Gary R. Collins, NavPress, Colorado Springs, p. 113
[20] *Baptist Psalmody: Selection of Hymns*, Basil Manly, Southern Baptist Publications Society, Charleston, SC, 1851, p. 683

Chapter 12

[21] *The Book of Church Growth*, Thom Rainer, Broadman & Holman Publishers, Nashville, 1993 p.183
[22] *Coach Wooden – One-On-One*, John Wooden and Jay Carty, Regal Press, Ventura, California, 2002, - Day 28, Praying to Win.
[23] *Pouring New Wine into Old Wine Skins*, Aubrey Malphurs, Baker Books, Grand Rapids, 1993, p. 165.
[24] *"The Leader As Change Agent"* - Doug Murren, *Leaders on Leadership*, George Barna, Regal Books, Ventura, CA, p. 201